LEGAL DISCLAIMER

The information contained in "Digital eCommerce Strategy" and its components, is meant to serve as a comprehensive collection of strategies that the author of this eBook has applied to making the ecommerce business sustainable and easier to start up. Summaries, strategies, tips and tricks are only recommendations by the author, and reading this eBook will not guarantee that one's results will exactly mirror the author's results.

The author of this eBook has made all reasonable efforts to provide current and accurate information for the readers of this eBook. The author and its associates will not be held liable for any unintentional errors or omissions that may be found.

The material in the eBook may include information by third parties. Third party materials comprise of opinions expressed by their owners. As such, the author of this eBook does not assume responsibility or liability for any third-party material or opinions.

The publication of third party material does not constitute the author's guarantee of any information, products, services or opinions contained within third party material. Use of third party material does not guarantee that your results will mirror our results. Publication of such third-party material is simply a recommendation and expression of the author's own opinion of that material.

Whether because of the progression of the Internet, or the unforeseen changes in company policy and editorial submission guidelines, what is stated as fact at the time of this writing may become outdated or inapplicable at a later date.

Great effort has been exerted to safeguard the accuracy and validity of this writing. Opinions regarding similar website platforms have been formulated as a result of both personal experience, as well as the well documented experiences of others.

© 2017 Raghu Ramasubbu

written expressed and signed permission from the author.

COPYRIGHT PAGE

DIGITAL eCOMMERCE STRATEGY – *Doing Business on the Internet* by Raghu Ramasubbu

© 2017 by Raghu Ramasubbu. All rights reserved.

TABLE OF CONTENT

LEGAL DISCLAIMER	1
COPYRIGHT PAGE	2
TABLE OF CONTENT	3
INTRODUCTION	5
NICHE SELECTION	8
WHAT EXACTLY IS A NICHE?	9
EXPLORING POPULAR SITES	12
USING GOOGLE TRENDS	15
CONSIDER YOUR PROMOTIONAL STRATEGIES	17
EVALUATING SEO	19
PRODUCT IDEAS	22
GENERATING PRODUCT IDEAS	23
EVALUATING PRODUCT IDEAS	26
DETERMINING YOUR MARKET SIZE	30
SOURCING FOR YOUR PRODUCTS	34

DEFINE YOUR MARKETING STRATEGY 40

IDENTIFYING YOUR TARGET CUSTOMER 42

EVALUATING THE COMPETITION 46

MAKING YOURSELF UNIQUE AMONG YOUR COMPETITORS 50

PROMOTIONAL METHODS TO USE 54

LAUNCHING YOUR ECOMMERCE STORE 63

ECOMMERCE PLATFORMS TO BUILD YOUR ONLINE STORE 64

STEPS TO DO AFTER CHOOSING YOUR DESIRED PLATFORM 75

POINTS TO CONSIDER TO LAUNCH YOUR FIRST ECOMMERCE WEBSITE 78

SCALING AND OPTIMIZE YOUR ECOMMERCE BUSINESS 82

MAKING YOURSELF A NICHE EXPERT 85

IMPROVING YOUR ECOMMERCE STORE 89

SOME THINGS TO AVOID 97

INTRODUCTION

In the digital age, many companies that were previously limited to brick and mortar have made the shift to also offering their consumers the option of buying their products online. This move makes a lot of sense since having an ecommerce store allows companies to seamlessly integrate actual selling points into their different marketing campaigns. The move does however remain a daunting one for many businesses since there are many technical aspects to consider.

The highly competitive ecommerce arena has begun to see an evolution in the paradigm of packages prices and shopping cart platforms. Many ecommerce management software providers are successfully bundling their ecommerce software with storefront templates, shopping carts, and complete marketing services making it easy for the inspired entrepreneur to start an online retail business.

While the internet itself always provided a revitalized, virtually unlimited opportunity for making money, there still existed - as with most pursuits - numerous challenges and a somewhat slippery learning curve. Foremost among the obstacles for excited proprietors and transitioning companies, is adapting an existing local retail business to the web: stores without stores, displays without bulky shelving comprised solely of pixels, customers service departments replaced by phone agents, and the unending yearning to create significant brand awareness in a market that had no regional boundaries. Meanwhile, before we proceed, it's necessary for us to define the term "Digital Ecommerce."

What is Digital eCommerce?

Digital commerce is the buying and selling of goods and services using the Internet, mobile networks and commerce infrastructure.

It includes the marketing activities that support these transactions, including people, processes and technologies to offer content, analytics, promotion, pricing, customer acquisition and retention, and customer experience at all touchpoints throughout the customer buying journey and experience.

ecommerce Solutions for the Digital World

The fast pace of the modern and digitally enabled world has put the internet at the centre of human interaction. Many transactions take place using the internet as companies and businesses have adapted to the World Wide Web for selling their products and services. Ecommerce simply means the buying and selling of products online. Crossing geographical boundaries and time zones, it is a continuous and constant medium for buying and selling worldwide.

So that the vast potential of the internet can be tapped and effectively utilized, ecommerce solutions such as payment gateways, shopping cart software, ecommerce websites such as Yahoo Stores now provide the much-needed impetus for online growth. Looking into the tremendous growth of ecommerce, many ecommerce solutions have become extremely popular. Some of these include Volusion, BigCommerce, Shopify, and 3DCart, Drupal, osCommerce, Zen-Cart, Joomla CMS, Dot Net Nuke, and others.

Ecommerce has demonstrated its global reach, and has given B2B and B2C interactions a great impetus. As ecommerce has developed rapidly, it has opened up the scope for businesses to develop rapidly and has narrowed down the barriers that existed previously between different countries and societies worldwide. Ecommerce solutions enable ecommerce websites to enhance the profile and corporate image of companies, while making it profitable for them to operate their business online.

Ecommerce solutions provide various tools to websites to enhance their visibility online and attract more customers to transact online. At the same time, it is easier for businesses to provide seamless shopping experience to customers, right from purchasing the product to making the payment and finally obtaining the delivery. Yet another dimension is to provide solutions to bring customers to the site in order to attract repeat business. The ultimate aim is to help the company generate more profits while providing quality shopping experience for the customers.

As living standards improve around the world, the way people buy is also changing. The internet provides a brilliant medium for channeling the buyer to the supplier and vice-versa. Ecommerce solutions provide a smooth way to facilitate such transactions and make the world of ecommerce better for the benefit of society.

Perhaps you are just wanting to setting up one or have an ecommerce business up and running or, and you would like to know the required steps and explore the various benefits of selling online. In this eBook, I'll walk you through on how to set up a profitable digital ecommerce taking into account tasks and considerations.

Let's begin!

NICHE SELECTION

How important is a niche for a beginner in digtal eCommerce? That depends on the type of approach you want to use and how you foresee your ability to meet a demand or fill a need. It's extremely easy to go into a business, particularly internet marketing. What's difficult is to stay afloat.

Looking for the perfect ecommerce niche idea is always hard. At the very beginning, you are overwhelmed with questions. What niche to think of? What to concentrate on? What if the chosen field won't turn out to be as profitable as expected?

It is typically recommended to choose a niche that suits your own interests and passions. That's a nice place to start, and that's a guarantee you will treat this business patiently and professionally.

Still, if you want to build a profitable eCommerce webstore, you need to base your niche choice upon some reliable and measurable criteria. Having a niche might just be your ticket to Web-based business success, provided you choose the right product or service to sell. Let's take a look at the benefits of choosing a niche for beginners in internet marketing and how you can, with careful considerations, find a place where you can truly shine.

WHAT EXACTLY IS A NICHE?

A niche is simply an area of the market that has a specialized need or want. It can vary in size, depending on the type of product and service being offered and on the preferences of the group itself. Niche marketing is simply the method of targeting the specific group of people or businesses that have a particular interest in the product or service you have to offer.

If you'll be offering a product, for example, you could design it in such a way that it meets a specific target. If the other businesses in your industry produce products for children and teens, you could, for example, offer products for 'tweens - that segment of the market that is halfway from being a child to being a teenager. Usually, this segment often gets left

© *2017 Raghu Ramasubbu*

behind when it comes to planning and designing products, giving way to the more popular market of children and teenagers. By targeting this segment of the market, you fill a gap that generally gets ignored by other businesses.

Choosing A Niche

As a beginner in internet marketing, it can be tempting to try covering more than one niche. There is nothing wrong with this. In fact, many internet marketers try their hands at several niches to identify which one is most feasible. This is also a way to zero in on the niche that is best for them.

You can, for example, cater to two different niche markets in the same industry or choose a niche market in two or more industries, depending on how well you can handle it. But how exactly do you choose which niche to focus on? We take a look at the options:

Your Interests, Skills And Passions Combined

Nothing beats working in a business you know something about and absolutely love. Probably a common denominator among all the men and women in the world who consider themselves successful are those that are not only good at what they do, but are also absolutely enamored with it, regardless of the type of industry they are in.

As a beginner in internet marketing, you can choose a niche by simply considering what you love best. Consider what you've always loved doing, what you did best, the kind of skill you can offer that has earned you recognition in the past, or just something you see yourself doing for years to come.

Your Resources

Some niche markets will cost you money to start. You'll have to spend for equipment, materials, labor and sometimes, research. Determine the kind of resources you have at hand and how much of it you're willing, or at least can afford, to spend. If you don't have enough, determine how and where you'll get additional capital.

A Need Nobody Noticed

A niche market, more than anything, caters to a unique need or requirement. When you choose your niche, consider the kind of needs that are out there that haven't been exactly met. Try to study the niche market you're considering and see what it needs that other business owners have not exactly offered products or services for.

Although choosing a niche market limits your target, it however creates a real possibility for you. The area may be small but it's real, capable of sustaining and even growing your business.

Managing The Niche

As a beginner in digital ecommerce marketing, prepare to multi-task. Choose a niche you can truly focus on, regardless of whether you decide to work in only one or five niches. Consider if marketing to this niche is feasible and determine what type of growth you can expect later. A niche may seem like the obvious choice to you but if there's no real market behind it or if the market is temporary at best, you might want to make some changes in your business plan.

A niche market that only has a seasonal demand, for example, means that you'll either have to make enough in order to cover for the lean months or at least have something else to fall back on. As an internet marketing beginner, it's important that you choose a niche you will enjoy working in and that allows you to build a business you can rely on in the future.

EXPLORING POPULAR SITES

When we select eCommerce niches for our own stores, we evaluate their potential with the help of several parameters.

First of all, we visit the website of the supplier we've previously chosen – most typically, it's a seller's store on sites like AliExpress. Here we can check the relevant statistics to see if this niche and the and the specific products you have chosen will be a good choice.

We use a five-star scale. The rating of 5 stars means that from the point of view of this separate parameter, this niche has an excellent potential. The rating of 1 star means that from the point of view of this separate parameter, this niche is not promising at all.

When we visit a supplier site (Aliexpress as Case Study), we estimate:

© **2017 Raghu Ramasubbu**

1. ***AliExpress products quantity***. We look at the number of items that can be found here upon the use of a particular keyword. We only include the items that have the free shipping option and the 4*+ rating.

—If we can find more than 2 000 items, the score we assign to this niche is 5*;
—For 500 – 1 999 items the score is 4,5*;
—For 100 – 499 items the score is 4*;
—For 1-99 items the score is 3*.

The niche popularity on AliExpress. We set the same parameters and sort the items by the number of orders. Then we take the first 10 items and calculate the arithmetic mean of the number of orders.

—If the arithmetic mean is more than 2000 orders, the score we assign to this niche is 5*;
—For 500 – 1999 orders the score is 4,5*;
—For 100 – 499 orders the score is 4*;
—For 1-99 orders the score is 3*.

2. **Trusted supplier**. We set the same parameters, take the first 10 stores, and evaluate them by the same parameters as AliExpress itself does:

—How long the store has been in operation;
—What its feedback score is;
—What the percentage of its positive feedback is;
—How much the items fit their descriptions;
—How good is the communication ;
—How satisfactory the shipping speed is.

We consider all these parameters, but, in our opinion, the percentage of positive feedback is the most important. Customer satisfaction is a key factor to a store's commercial success. This is why we calculate the arithmetic mean of the feedback score for these first 10 stores:

—If the arithmetic mean is more than 96%, the score we assign to this niche is 5*;
—For 95% – 95,9% the score is 4,5*;
—For 94% – 94,9% the score is 4*;
—For 93% – 93,9% the score is 3*.

3. **Price setting aspects**. We are surely most interested in the products and niches where a considerable markup is possible. It is exactly the case for the majority of simple basic goods offered on AliExpress because their prices are really low. It means there's no problem with setting a higher price on our drop shipping website – it will anyway be lower than the price of competitors' goods, so our customers will be satisfied with the purchase, and we will be happy with the profit.

To estimate the margin potential, we take the price of the most popular item in the niche and look this item up in 10 other online stores. We calculate the arithmetic mean of these 10 different prices (i.e. the average market price) and compare it to the price set by AliExpress seller.

—If the difference is more than 250%, the score we assign to this niche is 5*;
—For 100% – 249% the score is 4,5*;

—For 50% – 99% the score is 4*;
—For 1% – 49% the score is 3*.

USING GOOGLE TRENDS

Fashion, as well as public interest towards different product categories and separate items, tends to change over time. You need to monitor it if you want to be sure that people's interest on this niche is stable.

Google Trends is a powerful instrument that gives you the necessary insight into general public interest towards particular products. This service is designed to analyse search trends, so that it is beneficial to your business. Here are some trends that you want to look into.

—How is the search volume changes over time?
—What are the most popular search terms?
—Where are the people searching for this term live?
—Whether the interest towards this search is seasonal?

How to use it?

1. Pick a product category. The easiest way to do this is to rely on Aliexpress and gather all its possible categories (e.g. electronics, home and décor, jewellery, etc.).
2. Go to Google Trends and type in this category in the 'Explore Topics' field. Let's take 'knitting', for example.
3. Look at the result and try to analyze it using additional settings. For example, the graph produced shows how the search volume changes over time, and, as you can see, it decreases gradually.
4. To learn more about this dynamics, you can change some of the following settings:
   —Your region of interest;
   —Time frame;
   —Categories;
   —Type of content
   —If the trend is ascending, the score we assign to this niche is 5*;
   —For a flat trend the score is 4*;

—For a descending trend the score is 3*.

What's quite curious, this example shows the seasonal interest towards a search query. There are types of goods (for example, Halloween decorations, Christmas gifts, etc.) that are in demand only for a limited period of time. There's nothing wrong with having these products in your store if they are combined with some other kinds of offers (birthday cards, wedding decorations, etc.) that are not season-dependent, but it's not recommended to rely on them solely.

Surely, you will also find it essential to learn more about the geographical regions where this search query is the most popular.

Additionally, you will get the chance to see the most popular related search terms and estimate the speed of their popularity growth. This will be a very important piece of knowledge at the moment of planning your marketing and SEO strategies for promoting your eCommerce webstore.

CONSIDER YOUR PROMOTIONAL STRATEGIES

We should try to estimate if we can successfully promote our offers on various social networks, at least on such popular ones as Facebook and Instagram.

For example, while evaluating whether we can use Instagram for a particular category, we use the statistics provided by the Websta service. All you need to do is type the chosen category in the 'Search' field.

Having done that, the search results are divided into two categories: users who have this keyword in their account names, and hashtags with this keyword. Therefore you can easily understand:

—What kinds of hashtags you need to use in order to reach the widest possible audience (these numbers show how many times the hashtag was used);

—What user accounts you can cooperate with in order to increase your webstore awareness.

To evaluate how promising this niche is, we use the following criteria:

—If there are more than 10 accounts with more than 30 000 followers, the score we assign to this niche is 5*;
—For 5-9 accounts the score is 4,5*;
—For 1-4 accounts the score is 4*;
—For 0 accounts with this amount of followers the score is 3*.

We usually try to collaborate with the accounts that have at least 30,000 followers as this provides us with quite a significant audience. The most common way of such collaboration is promotion via shoutouts: we ask the account owner to publish our advertising posts from time to time on a paid basis.

When evaluating the promotional potential of a drop shipping niche, don't forget about Facebook! Facebook as a social network is an exciting tool to communicate with your prospects and make your webstore well-known and popular.

To check whether the chosen niche has the necessary potential, type its name in the 'Search' field and choose the 'Groups' section. You will see a list of the existing groups that have this keyword in their names, and member count.

We usually consider a niche to be promising and prospective if it has more than 15 groups with more than 30,000 members per each. Additionally, it can be useful to also check out the 'Pages' section – it gives you even more insight into this niche popularity and its opportunities for your business.

—If there are more than 10 groups with more than 30 000 members, the score we assign to this niche is 5*;

—For 5-9 groups the score is 4,5*;

—For 1-4 groups the score is 4*;

—For 0 groups with this amount of subscribers the score is 3*.

It's important to mention that all these parameters can be successfully used to evaluate not only these particular niches, but the related ones as well. For example, exploring the knitting niche, you can also consider looking into sewing and knitting patterns, craftwork materials, etc.

It is also a great strategy to choose a product category that can easily be promoted through pay-per-click advertising and search engine optimization tools. It means that we check if:

—We can generate valuable content for the niche in question;

—Be able to optimize images and videos;

—We can select enough relevant and competitive keywords related to this category.

This is why search engine optimization (SEO) is vital for a successful webstore promotion.

EVALUATING SEO

There are several important points you need to research before making up your mind on any niche for your eCommerce business.

To make the eCommerce niche evaluation easier for you, we have created a scale that will help you decide which products have more potential in terms of SEO, and which ones are not feasible.

The first step is keywords analysis.

Every niche name is in fact a keyword. Therefore, first of all you should estimate the number of searches for this keyword on Google (and for those that sound alike). You can do it with Google Keyword Planner.

© 2017 Raghu Ramasubbu

If a keyword has something between 10K and 100K searches, it is the perfect category for a drop shipping niche, as it has some demand but it doesn't exceed the sensible limits. If there are more than 100K searches, the niche is too wide and the competition will be simply huge and challenging. If there are less than 5K searches, skip to the next niche option: this one probably has neither competition nor profit.

We personally rate the results the following way:

- —If there are 5K-50K searches, the score we assign to this drop shipping niche is 5* since it's perfect in terms of competition;
- —For 50K-100K the score is 4* – the competition is great, but there still might be a place for you;
- —For ≤ 5K searches the score is 3* – the niche is all yours, but there's no profit in it;
- —For ≥ 100K the score is 2* – the competition is too high, no chances to win.

You can see that Google Keyword Planner has only 3 ranges, therefore we advise you to look through the list of related keywords it provides for your query. If there are a lot of keywords with 10-100K searches, it is probably between 50-100K in our scale; if there are mostly 1-10K, it is closer to 5K-50K in our scale.

During the next step, you need to conduct a manual research and get an insight into the niche and your probable competitors. In order to do that, open Google search page, enter the following query in the search field and click "search":

allinurl:niche name (for example: allinurl:knitting)

As the result, Google will show you the pages that have that keyword in their URL, which is a competitive advantage for them. Look at the number of pages Google shows and that will give you a rough idea of the competition in the niche.

We personally rate the results the following way:

—If there are 10K-100K pages, the score we assign to this niche is 5* since it's perfect in terms of competition;

—For 3K-10K pages the score is 4* – you'll have to work hard to win the competition but it will be worth it;

—For ≤ 3K pages the score is 3* – the competition is pretty low but profits are not high;

—For ≥ 100K the score is 2* – the competition is too high, no chances to win.

We can also recommend using special services like Keyword Explorer by Moz. You'll need to register with Moz and you'll be granted access to this tool.

Just enter your keyword to the search field and click "try free". This wonderful tool will estimate the keyword competition in real figures and provide extremely valuable information on the competition for a niche.

Moz analyses whether it's difficult to work effectively in such a competition, shows your opportunities and the potential of entering this niche. Even though all these criteria are crucial, we first of all look at the "Difficulty" parameter as it lets us know if the competition in this niche is good for us. We personally rate the results the following way:

> —If "Difficulty" reaches the mark of 0-40, the score we assign to this niche is 5*;
> —For 41-60 the score is 4*;
> —For 61-80 pages the score is 3*;
> —For 81-100 the score is 2*.

We advise you to research everything this tool suggests. But remember that this is a limited version since it's free, however it is exactly enough to evaluate a few niche options.

The last step of our evaluation is the manual analysis of search engine results pages. To understand your potential SEO competition with huge retailers, just enter your niche keyword in Google search field and explore the results on the first 2 pages.

If the whole first page is taken by such behemoths as Amazon, eBay and others – there is a really slim chance that you will have any profit in this niche. It will be really hard to compete with these giants who get 90% of all the customers. What is left brings no profit. The only other option is whether you can sell the product at a much lower price than what these retailers are bringing in, and maybe you have a chance.

If the results include not your competitors but some services like Yahoo!Answers or some spammy articles (such resources are called Easy Target), this means that the niche or product has a chance for you to take it on.

—If the 1st page is mainly taken by giants but there are up to 4 places taken by Easy Target results, the score we assign to this niche is 5* – this is the most preferable result where you can get a good spot in the competition and enjoy decent profits;

—If the 1st page is fully taken by giants, the score is 4* – the competition is extremely high and your chances are rather slim;

—If the majority of the results on the 1st page are Easy Target, the score is 3* – you can win the competition but profits won't be worth it;

—If the 1st and 2nd pages are taken by giants, the score is 2* – your chances for a commercially successful venture are insignificantly low.

PRODUCT IDEAS

Picking the best products to sell is the next big challenge after deciding to start your eCommerce venture. There are millions of products to choose from, and all of them have had success. This is why picking products can be extremely difficult which can lead to products being picked on a whim, with little consideration, which ends in poor performance.

There are many ways to generate ideas for best selling products on the Internet. In this chapter, our goal is to provide a roadmap for brainstorming product ideas, so we can later filter out the ones that aren't worth looking into.

GENERATING PRODUCT IDEAS

Brainstorm

You never start with a blank page. Your head is already full of good ideas: your hobbies, products you like, trends, exciting products that you have heard of. Write everything down that comes to mind. It doesn't matter if you think the product will be a bestseller or not. Trust me — write it down.

Browse Other Shops

When you browse other stores, look at their offerings, best selling lists, and promoted products. Many stores have a tremendous amount of data and employ entire departments to organize their sales and pick their products. Use that information to your benefit.

—Browse a lot.
—Browse frequently.

Here is a list that is worth spending time researching

- —AliExpress Most Popular Products (Weekly)
- —Amazon Best Sellers
- —Ebay Daily Deals
- —Lazada Top Sellers
- —LightInTheBox Top Sellers List

Forums

Forums are real "idea hangouts". You can pick out many winning ideas just from a 10-minute visit to a popular forum. After all, forums are places where the target market meet to discuss their hobbies and their passion. Look out for hot questions and recurring themes.

Magazines

Magazines! These popular items are great for browsing through and getting instant ideas. See ads which always seem to run every month? That means those ads are profitable, or the advertiser won't be continuously running them! Use these ads as a springboard for some hot products you can create.

Google Hot Trends

Here's a secret site to get tons of killer ideas in an instant: Google Hot Trends at google.com/trends. This site keeps tracks of the hottest Internet searches in the last few hours. It's a great site to keep in touch with what's "In" at the moment.

Browse Social Shopping Sites

There are over 100 million products on Polyvore and 30 million on Wanelo. Add in Fancy and Pinterest, and you now have an infinite number of products from around the world that can be sorted by popularity, trends, categories, and more. People often overlook these sites in their research, but they are very valuable. Set up an account at each one, and subscribe to different categories and lists. Follow what people like the most and add it to your list.

Ask Friends

The next time you have coffee with friends, ask their thoughts on trends. Don't limit yourself — talk with friends of all ages and backgrounds to get a wide variety of ideas.

Look Around

Look around your house, your work, your life. Are there any products you can't live without? What products would make your life easier? Is there anything that is hard to find in the supermarket or department store? Howard Schultz came up with his coffee shop idea on a trip to Italy and later called it Starbucks. The founder of Inkkas brought his idea from Peru, where he saw great shoes he thought that people in the US would like.

Stay alert and spot opportunities. You see hundreds of products and ideas each day. Be observant, carry a notebook, and remember to write everything down.

EVALUATING PRODUCT IDEAS

As you may have noticed, generating the product ideas is the easy part. What truly matters is knowing which products will sell well, or at least have the potential. In this chapter, we will narrow down our ideas list and decide which products we are going to sell in our eCommerce store. There are eight different filters. Go through each one and eliminate ideas that fail to meet the criteria.

Filtering Product Ideas

1. **Niche Filter**: With the rise of dropshipping and the relative ease that an eCommerce store can be created, niche shops have become the trend. It quickly turned from an eCommerce novelty to a proven, successful strategy. Don't fight the big stores. Avoid too broad and general categories. The masses are already exposed to thousands of offers daily.

Look to supply niche products that are underserved by larger players. For example, there is no specific interest group for a normal belt, but you can easily tell that cycling gear will resonate well with cycling enthusiasts. Find your niche.

2. **Stay Away Categories Filter**: It may overlap with the Niche Filter, but it's essential to narrow down your product selections by excluding the 'stay away' categories.

Some product categories have grown significantly over the last decade, so there are already many strong players and smaller shops out there supplying these products. Just look at the eCommerce growth rates: book sales are flat and the jewelry market is shrinking. 80% of Americans say they've bought electronics or apparel online in the past three months, which means they already have their choice of trusted store.

Cross off the following general categories from your idea list: books, jewelry, electronics, and clothing — you will need to be more specific and find a niche.

Please note: I don't suggest crossing out these categories entirely. You could sell plus size women's clothing, men's clothing, custom hiking/cycling electronics gear, or jewelry hidden in candles. I suggest you focus on finding an interesting subcategory that will make your store unique. Don't fall into the trap of selling in general categories.

3. **Price Sweet Spot Filter:** We found that the perfect eCommerce product price is $40 to $60 (at a 200% mark-up). With a $40 to $60 price range, the profits are relatively good and you can still cover the marketing costs of up to $20 per sale.

The conversion rate is usually higher because the purchase requires less consideration on the part of the buyer. There is also less support. You increase the odds of the success of your store in the developing markets. With Chinese dropshipping, you can sell everywhere in the world. Although $30 may not be much to people living in the US, but it could be a lot for someone in South America or Eastern/Central Europe.

Look over your list and cross out product ideas that are more than $60.

4. **Marketing Channels Filter:** You have to think about your marketing strategy before you even launch your store. You may change it, but you must have a plan to begin with.

To put it simply, different marketing channels are great for different products. Once you pick the product, you have to figure out which marketing channel will be best for it. Advertising an $800 hoverboard on Facebook might not be the best idea, but you might succeed in advertising it on Google Adwords. A hoverboard is not a spontaneous purchase, in most cases people will Google it to learn more about it and find which stores sell it.

Think about your resources (time, money, knowledge), select one or two marketing channels, and cross out all ideas that don't suit those channels.

5. **Google Trends & Keyword Tools:** This is a must if you're going to use Google Adwords or if you're trying to grow your organic traffic. I recommend using these even if you're going to use another marketing channel. It helps to see what products are trending and also to check the demand of your product ideas.

Go through your product ideas and enter each product name and their variations into the Google Keywords Analysis tool. Select Keywords Ideas method and look at how many searches each Low Competition Keyword receives.

Let's say you could get all of that traffic and 2% of them would buy at your store. Would this demand be enough?

Next, go to trends.google.com and do the same. Enter each of your product ideas into the search and look what the trend is. Is the trend increasing or decreasing? Are there any patterns? Do you see any spikes?

What Does It All Mean? In general, you should avoid product categories that have little or no search traffic (less than 500 monthly searches). If you are planning to do a lot of search campaigns or grow organically through SEO, you should further dismiss all product ideas that have high competition according to the Google Keyword Analysis Tool.

6. **Seasonality Filter**: Avoid seasonal products like Christmas decorations, Easter baskets, and even children's toys. You can check product seasonality trends at Google Trends.

By focusing on seasonal items, you are reducing your sales cycle. Most Christmas decoration sales do not take place in the spring or summer, and Easter basket sales are not high in the fall or winter. You want to put products in your store that will be attractive for buyers for the entire year.

7. **Copyrights Filter**: Dismiss all branded products — it is not easy to find suppliers. If you dropship them from little-known suppliers, chances are you'll be selling fake products. Build your own shop brand, and avoid western brands.

8. **Competition Filter**: Evaluating your competition may be an endless task, but you need to check whether the product you're about to start advertising is already widespread among other websites.

Here's a simple trick, most store owners will likely have the same images. Google a product and try doing a product image search. Look at how many shops have similar products. Find your competitors, check their pricing strategy, research their popularity/traffic (on sites like Alexa.org or SpyFu.com), and what marketing channels they are using. Cross out all products ideas that already have huge competition.

DETERMINING YOUR MARKET SIZE

Once you have decided what kind of products you are going to sell, you next need to determine how big the market is for those products. There are a number of mistakes that some new entrepreneurs make when setting up their store for the first time. We'll go over a few of those in a moment. If you can avoid the mistakes, then you have a much better chance of being successful. Determining market size definitely is one of the most important things that you can do before setting up your store, but do keep mind that even if you determine that the market is too small for the product that you have chosen, you might still be able to sell it.

That's one of the first mistakes that people make when they are determining their market size. They stubbornly stick to one product because it is their passion and that's why they got into the business in the first place. There's nothing wrong with that, except that if you want to be successful, you are going to have to do more than sell a product that almost no one wants. So, how do you do you appeal to a wider customer base while still selling something that you are familiar with or knowledgeable about. There are actually two ways that this can be accomplished.

Expand Your Product Line

So, you want to sell bandanas or 'do rags that feature horses. This is a great product for someone who wants to wear a bandana that features horses. But there aren't many people looking for that particular product. In fact, you might be hard-pressed to sell a single bandanna. But there is definitely a market for 'do rags and bandannas. The problem is, there is too much competition in this wider market, which is why you went with the niche – that and your unparalleled expertise on horse prints and patterns of course. But what if you decided to sell bandannas that featured all kinds of animal, pop culture and photo print designs. You suddenly have opened yourself up to a huge market of bandanna and 'do rag wearing customers.

Learn Something New

Okay, so maybe your niche product only appeals to a very specific niche and there isn't anything you can do to expand it. You don't want to stick with that niche on a potentially huge ecommerce site like your Shopify site. Instead, you want to learn something new. Simply move on to a new niche and if you don't know anything about it, then you can learn before you open your store. Of course, you can always find something that is related to your original niche idea so that you can at least incorporate the products that you had in mind at some later date when you have already established a name for yourself with the new niche.

Don't be Afraid to Choose a Large Market

Another mistake that budding entrepreneurs make when they are first setting up their store is to balk at competing in a large market. If you are looking at your market and feeling fearful that you will get lost in the shuffle, take heart. There are actually several things that you can do to distinguish yourself in a large market to make sure that you can compete with the big guys. We'll go over those strategies in a later chapter.

How to Determine the Size of a Market

So, how do you determine the size of a market for a product that you are considering selling? The first step is to check out the market research that has already been done for you. There is no reason not to take advantage of information that is provided by the government, not-for-profit organizations or even companies that have released the information. To determine the size of the market you'll research your industry with the Small Business Administration or through FedStats.gov. There are also organizations devoted to each industry that will have more accurate numbers. Checking out these numbers is the first step in determining market size, but not the last one, because you are likely competing in a niche market within that consumer segment.

Determine Your Niche Market

Please refer to the previous section where we discussed about niche selection. If you are competing in a niche market then you are going to want to narrow down the market segment that you figured out by researching the industry into a much smaller number, because you aren't likely to find specific numbers on your particular niche unless it is incredibly broad. For example, if you are selling bandanas, you wouldn't be able to get numbers on how many people buy bandanas and 'do rags but you might be able to get specific numbers on how many people in the country are buying health and beauty products – hint: it's almost all of them. That's unfortunately how the numbers are structured. Luckily there are some solid ways to narrow down your market and be fairly accurate.

Demographics

We're going to go into demographics in detail in the next chapter. But we'll have to skip ahead just a little to make a point here. In order to narrow down your niche market, you're going to have to read chapter three and follow the instructions there, because you can't have one without the other. Your ideal customer will determine what demographics you look at, and that will determine what your market size is going to be. As for the demographics that make up your ideal customers, that will be up to you based upon your research.

Estimating Market Size by Competition

Another way that you can estimate the market size of the niche that you are going to be working in is by looking at the competition. For example: if you were to go to Amazon and look at their book selection under the 'Arts & Photography' category, you will notice that while 'Architecture' has more than 10,000 books in that subcategory, the subcategory 'Dance' only has about 1000. That means that you can safely assume that the dance book niche is about 10% of the size of the architecture book niche. You don't have to use Amazon for this method, but if you can, it is usually pretty accurate.

If you don't want to use Amazon's listings, or your particular niche isn't represented there, you can use the search engines with the same effect. For example: suppose that you were selling bandannas with famous movie stars on them. If you were to type in 'bandanas' you could check out the competition that comes up and see how many of them (if any) are offering movie star bandanas.

Even better, if you have a Google account, you can use the Adwords Keyword Planner to type in phrases that will allow you to see just how many people search monthly for a particular keyword phrase. For example, you might type in 'Tiger print bandanas' and see that more than 1000 people every month search for that particular item. That means that if you sold tiger print bandanas and you could get your website in front of those people, you'd make some sales.

So, determining your market size isn't that difficult. But it's not all that accurate either, unless you willing to spend tens of millions on market research.

SOURCING FOR YOUR PRODUCTS

Congrats, you've gotten through the most critical first step of starting an online store selecting the perfect products to sell. Also, If you're just starting out with e-commerce business, it is inevitable that you will come across the fact that your customers want more choices when it comes to products that are sold online. People want to visit the online store, and they want to choose between hundreds of perfectly categorized and neatly priced products. But the thing is, it's not always that easy to find an appealing plethora of products that you can offer in your online store. That's where developing e-commerce product sourcing strategy steps in.

How to Source and Manufacture Products for

Your eCommerce Business

You have three primary sourcing options to consider. No option is inherently better than another, but there are a variety of factors to weigh when determining which works best for your business and for you.

1. DIY Products or Services

The idea of crafting your own product dates back centuries. Today, thanks to the internet, you now have a much wider reach for selling handmade goods.

But if you're thinking about creating your own products, there are some factors to consider.

Perks and Pitfalls: You will have full control over your brand and will likely be coming into the space with something new. Startup costs are typically low, although you're going to need to put time and energy into your business, which is a sacrifice in and of itself. You'll want to make sure you're always thinking ahead about how you will scale and possibly grow your product line over time in order to stay competitive and offer your customer base something new.

Tasks to Get Started:

—Source materials: It could be from your local flea market, craft stores, estate sales, an established retailer or even friends and family. Identify your materials, where you'll get them and how much they'll cost.

—Determine how you'll ship orders: Will you be running to the post office or UPS store yourself, or would hiring a shipping service be worth saving time and energy?

—Learn what it will take to ship: Give thought to packaging, since it will have downstream effects on total costs and could create shipping challenges later on.

—Calculate how long your products take to make: You should know exactly how long it takes to make a product. Also give some thought as to whether or not you will make items to order or if you want to keep inventory on hand. Be sure to document any labor costs, whether it's money spent or time spent.

—Consider where you'll store your inventory: Even if you're lucky enough to have an empty room in your home, that probably won't scale with your business. Look into alternatives like renting a space, opening a storefront or using 3PL.

—Make a plan for communicating timelines: Your website should set expectations on how long it takes to craft a product and complete an order. You can do this in places like your product description and shipping and returns policy, plus reiterate in your transactional emails. It's always better to be transparent and upfront so your shoppers feel confident purchasing from you.

2. Working with a Manufacturer or Wholesaler

Working with a manufacturer or wholesaler means you're essentially hiring a partner to develop your product. This is a great option if you aren't able to make a product yourself, or when you're ready to scale your DIY product by hiring someone else to make it for you, or to supplement for higher than planned sales.

Perks and Pitfalls: While this gives you the option to pursue a unique idea or sell popular products without making anything yourself, you may need to invest more heavily upfront. You can still have control over your brand and the quality of your product, plus get a great deal of assistance with production.

Items to Consider:

—Finding products: This can be as simple as forming a business relationship with a friend who makes a product you'd like to sell, partnering with an existing company and taking their business online or from B2B to B2C, hiring a manufacturer, building relationships with makers on Instagram or using Etsy Wholesale. If you're looking for a manufacturer to make your products, you can easily research options online. Finding the right partner can take some time, so don't get discouraged.

—Checking references: As with any business, you need to make sure you're dealing with someone who is legit. Reach out to others who have used the manufacturer or wholesaler, and maybe do a little digging at the Better Business Bureau. It's a good sign if the company you're researching asks for information that proves that you have a legitimate business, too. Be prepared to provide necessary licences or tax information.

—Evaluating your options: Be sure to ask questions of each company you're considering so you can make the best decision.

- What will the total cost be? Take into consideration production, shipping and potential hidden fees.
- How long will it take for them to make/ship the product?
- What does shipping and inventory management look like? Will you need to ship and store or is that included as part of their service? Is there any additional

cost? What are the timelines and conditions? Do you have control over package branding?

- What do the contracts and terms look like? Is there any wiggle room for things your business or customers need? Is there an evaluation period or terms for termination?
- What do support and communication look like? How frequently will you be updated on information like inventory, product changes or even discounts?
- What are the minimum order quantities? Will you have to commit to a certain number of units or spend a minimum amount?

—Getting a sample: Before you sign on with anyone, make sure their products meet your expectations. While some manufacturers will charge a fee to send you a sample, you can often negotiate a deal to only pay for it if you keep it.

—Picking one: Weigh your options and get going! You want to ensure you're making a smart decision, but that doesn't mean you should sit in research mode forever. Worst case, you pivot and go another direction.

3. Hiring a Dropshipper

Dropshipping is a method of product sourcing that lets you purchase from a vendor and list their products on your online store. The vendor charges you for the products as they are sold, and typically ships orders on your behalf.

It's a great option for starting a new online business, but is also good for expanding the product catalog of an existing store.

Perks and Pitfalls: Dropshipping means you don't need to deal with inventory, packaging or fulfilment. The catch is that you'll typically have more competition, as many of the products offered by dropshippers are readily available all over the internet. However, most have a wide selection of products from which you can choose. Dropshipping usually gives you a lower profit margin, so you'll need to sell a lot before making a good profit.

Items to Consider:

The steps to find a dropshipper or aggregate dropshipper (a dropshipper that works with a variety of dropshippers for you) are nearly the same as those you'd follow for the manufacturing option.

—Find some options
—Check their references
—Evaluate all of your options
—Ask for samples
—Pick one and go

3 Easy Steps to Develop Your E-commerce

Product Sourcing Strategy

You will face some challenges first like searching for the right products, making the right choices when it comes to manufacturing and offering quality products within your e-commerce store overall. You will also realize that having a product sourcing strategy will create a huge relieve in your efforts of building a successful online e-commerce business.

The next 3 tips will help you meet your product sourcing goals that you've set for your e-commerce store.

1. **Don't limit yourself to the same products over and over**

Yes, we should do what we do best. And yes, once a product is successful and proven, we should not change a thing, right?

When it comes to product sourcing, it's a whole different world out there. If a product sells well on your store, it's highly likely that the same product sells itself good on the other e-commerce stores too.

This is one of the main reasons why so many businesses are not online, and brick and mortar stores fail as well. They think that the same proven solutions and products will sell in the same channel forever. You can't keep up in the business world with that attitude and expect to grow the business.

You must always look for new products to sell them in your e-commerce store. By doing that, your e-commerce store will always stay relevant, up-to-date and attractive towards your target customers. And that directly results in increased profits overall.

2. **Always do a research before you decide what products to offer**

You may have some products that are bought on a frequent basis. But you can't expect that to be the case with every other product that you're selling in your e-commerce store. Every product will not become a best seller.

That's why, it is crucial to source a product that will be attractive for your target customers and that comes with an excellent price that the customers can pay. Before you decide what products to offer on your e-commerce store, you need to conduct market research first to see if your target customers are actually going to love the products or not.

3. Adopt successful product sourcing approaches

The competition for success in the e-commerce business is intense and rough. Every e-commerce business wants to be different from the competitors, and everyone wants bigger profit than the competitors.

This doesn't mean that e-commerce businesses shouldn't learn from each other and from the most successful product sourcing models in the market. There is nothing inappropriate in researching how the more successful competitors in the market do their product sourcing and learn from them. You don't have to disrupt the market here or something. It just takes a solid product sourcing approach.

To conclude, finding the right product manufacturers and product suppliers in the market is hard. Especially for e-commerce businesses. The product sourcing tips that are given above can help you unfold a product sourcing strategy that will work for your e-commerce business. By developing a solid product sourcing strategy, you will satisfy your target customer's taste and needs, and increase your profits in the process.

To have progressive growth, arguably you need a great product. However, for a great product, you need a stable and reliable supplier. Making a mistake at this point can be devastating for your business and reputation. Please note that, as with anything, there are always fringe cases. Don't get discouraged or give up on an idea just because it doesn't fit into any of the above scenarios. These are intended to serve as a guide to help you begin research and bubble up your most profitable and realistic business ideas.

DEFINE YOUR MARKETING STRATEGY

Running an integrated ecommerce marketing strategy is very important to your overall business goals and objectives. This strategy should incorporate all facets of your offline marketing and direct traffic to your site for lead generation and sales creation.

This necessitates auditing all your offline business materials to ensure that the web address is correctly referenced and considered. Most businesses that use the web as a serious marketing medium should have a formalized internet marketing strategy. This written

© *2017 Raghu Ramasubbu*

document should define the marketing objectives, state the planned intentions and provide a basis for measuring or benchmarking progress.

Ecommerce merchants face a ton of competition in achieving high search engine visibility for keyword phrases that prospective customers are searching for. That's the harsh reality of getting noticed and making sales on the World Wide Web. The good news is that with a little research, planning, and follow-though, the goal of moving ahead of the competition and generating some targeted Internet traffic becomes surprisingly attainable.

Building an ecommerce website and then getting it indexed by Google is the first hurdle in gaining visibility on the Internet and attracting a decent number of credit card wielding customers. But with thousands, if not millions of other ecommerce merchants clamoring for the attention of the same online customers, how does the little guy on the Web stand a snowball's chance? Well, the beauty of ecommerce marketing is that there are no "little guys"

-- only website owners who don't know the basics of search engine optimization, web design, and sales conversion principles.

Wait a minute! What was that last thing -- sales conversion principles? Is that something I need to go back to college for? Fortunately, no advanced degrees are necessary, although continual self-education is highly recommended! The main skill you need to convert web site visitors to customers is imagination -- if you could call that a "skill". To sell stuff to people on or off the Web, you need to have the ability to see things through their eyes. Stop being an e-marketer for a few seconds, and try to imagine what a first-time visitor to your site is going to see, think, and feel. Will their first impressions be that you're trying to sell them something? That, of course, is your intention, but keep in mind that ecommerce is a two-way street; people aren't going to buy what you're selling unless several conditions are met; and the art of written persuasion is definitely part of this ecommerce marketing strategy.

IDENTIFYING YOUR TARGET CUSTOMER

The next thing that you're going to have to do is identify the customer that you are trying to connect with. You've got a product niche all picked out and you've determined that the market size is sufficient to allow you to make money in said niche, but what about the actual person that is going to buy that product? You can't market to a faceless crowd. You need to know who is most likely to buy your product or use your service so that you can tailor your marketing specifically for them and entice them to buy from you. Understanding your ideal customer starts with a basic understanding of how demographics work.

Demographics: How to Know Which Group to

Market to

Some companies couldn't live without demographic data. That is the only way that they can make decisions, create marketing strategies and plan elaborate ad campaigns. To be fair, we are talking about tens or even hundreds of millions of dollars invested in some cases so it is no wonder that they evaluate their marketing plan carefully before they implement it. But for the average ecommerce website that specializes in a particularly niche, market data isn't a necessity. It is however, extremely useful. But to understand the data, you first have to understand how the groups are divided.

Demographic Attributes

To understand what sort of factors make up your target consumer, you need to understand what sort of categories that the experts divide people into. Here are just some of those categories.

—Men
—Women
—Men & Women 18-24
—Men & Women 35 to 34
—Men & Women 35 to 54
—Men & Women Age 55 and Over
—Level of education
—Size of the Household vs Ethnicity
—Race vs Income
—Occupation

So, you can see that identifying the ideal customer is a little more complicated than it looks on the surface and what goes into actually getting that information is even more difficult to understand. There are of course, some products for which demographics can be easily identified. For example: if you were marketing tampons, you'd want to market them exclusively to women between the ages of puberty and menopause. If you were marketing cologne on the other hand, you might market the same basic age groups for men on the other side.

However, other information is harder to come by. When a company wants to know who is more apt to buy their product, they have several ways to get the information. The most common one is paying for surveys. You might even have worked at one of these survey centers if you are part of Generation Y. Now, they are pretty much obsolete as the internet has made it incredibly easy to collect data. Companies spend millions tracking consumers as they shop, as they window shop and as they search for things that they'd rather not have Wal-Mart know about. Of course, this data is compiled and separated, and usually tells companies with a great deal of accuracy what kind of person is looking for the products that they sell.

Unfortunately, this method doesn't usually work for the average consumer, particularly not one just starting their own Shopify store. So, your method will have to be a little different. Even if you have no clue whatsoever who will be buying your products right now, there are some ways that you can identify your target consumer. Here are some tips.

How Small Businesses & Ecommerce Sites Can

Identify Their Target Market

The first thing that we're going to do is refer back to the beginning of this book. Remember the problem that you are solving? Well, that's the first step to identifying your target customer. What kind of person would be having the kind of problem that your product or service solves? From there you can begin to narrow things down a little bit. Is that person more likely to be male or female? What age range is this person apt to be in? Questions like these can help you begin to define your ideal audience.

Create a Picture of the Customer(s) in Your Head

Remember, your ideal customer doesn't have to be limited to just one person. You can create an archetype that encompasses several different age ranges, genders or income brackets. The important thing is that you create a picture of these customers in your head – in other words that you actually consider these customers to be real people and not just faceless cardboard cutouts in front of computer screens. Make an actual list of the customers you think that your product is right for, and divide them up by demographics like gender, age group and location.

See the Value in Your Product or Service

If you are having trouble narrowing down just what your ideal customer is going to be then you might need to ask yourself some defining questions to identify who would consider your product or service to be valuable. Here are some questions that you can use to paint a picture if you had trouble with this in the previous step.

—What is the problem again and what type of person is likely to suffer the most from it?
—If the customer does not deal with this problem using your product or service, what will the result be? What will happen if they fail to act?

Understand Your Market

Obviously, you are going to be a niche provider. Every small ecommerce company is a niche provider these days. The world of internet marketing and eCommerce is one that requires a niche in order to compete, and the more specialized a niche the better (assuming there is a market for it). Identifying your ideal customer requires that you understand your market intimately. Can you imagine if Roy Raymond had never been married or tried to buy his wife lingerie? Would Victoria's Secret have been as successful as it is? Raymond was able to compete in the industry and grow his company to be the world's largest intimate clothing retailer.

Up until that point, no one had thought of marketing lingerie to men. It was inconceivable. After all, men didn't wear lingerie. But Raymond discovered that the ideal customer was just like him and obviously, since he knew himself intimately, it was quite easy for him to begin marketing to his ideal customer. He created the perfect situation for himself to be successful – identifying who was most likely to buy his products and then laser targeting his marketing efforts towards them. That's not to say that Victoria's Secret didn't target women as well – they did – but at the time marketing lingerie to men was revolutionary – and it made Roy Raymond rich.

Understand Your Customer's Options

The previous example is also a demonstration of this principle. What options does the ideal customer have? This will help you decide who the ideal customer is, because you want them to have no option other than yourself. That's why the aforementioned Victoria's Secret was able to become the number one lingerie retailer in America. Men had no other option when it came to buying lingerie, except visiting the same stores that they had become embarrassed in and likely were unable to complete their purchases.

EVALUATING THE COMPETITION

Unless you truly are in the equine bandanna niche, you are going to have competition and probably a lot of it. But it's not as scary as it sounds. In fact, most of the people out there are floundering in their new ecommerce business just like you are, and even the ones who have their doo-doo together you can learn something from. So, just because there are others competing in your same niche, don't think that you aren't going to be able to compete. Instead, look at it as a challenge and more importantly, think of something unique that you can do or provide that would make people want to come and shop with you.

How to Know Who the Competition is

If you want to evaluate the competition, you first need to know who that competition is. If you sell tennis shoes, you can bet that the athletic stores, department stores, smaller online shoe sellers and discount websites will all be your competition. Even if you don't sell shoes, you can pretty much count on

© *2017 Raghu Ramasubbu*

Amazon competing with you on just about every real-world product you can think of. There are only a few pies that they haven't gotten their fingers in yet, and it is only a matter of time.

But what if you sell something that isn't so easy to define the competition for? Well, let's go back to the trusty bandana, aka 'do rag. Some people also call them scarves and both men and women wear them, usually on their head. A quick search in Google will show you that some of the top competitors for 'bandana' are some pretty well-known realworld stores like Hobby Lobby and Michaels. Of course, Amazon is at the top of the search results for this particular term. They usually are.

Luckily, you aren't trying to compete for bandanas. You're going to make a list of keywords that people use when they are searching for a particular type of bandana. To learn what people are typing in, you have two tried-and-true methods. The first is the Google Auto-Complete method.

Using Google Instant to Identify Your Products &

Competitors

If you have Google instant search (also known as auto-complete) turned on then you'll be able to see suggestions as you type. It's like Google is convinced that you don't know what you're trying to type into the search field. Even so, it makes a great way for you to see what people are looking for, and afterward, to see what companies are providing those products.

So, if you were to use Google Instant Search when it came to bandanas, you might begin by typing in the word 'bandana.' Unfortunately, this example doesn't lend itself well to demonstration because most of the descriptive terms that would narrow down your bandana selection appear before the word, not after. However, you can still use Google Instant to come up with some ideas by typing in a descriptive phrase and the word 'bandana' and then seeing what else comes up. For instance, if you were to type 'tiger stripe bandana' into Google Instant, you might notice that 'camo bandana' comes up a lot.

Once you have determined some of the keywords that describe products similar to those that you're going to be selling, your next step is to see who is selling under those keywords. It is important to distinguish that while you can use this method to come up with keywords for your own site or even for you to come up with a particular niche product to sell, the goal here is simply to see what kind of competitors are in the field by using related keywords. Ideally, you aren't going to find very many (read: hopefully none) competitors that are selling exactly what you are, but if you look at some of the related products you'll be able to develop a picture of the competition.

Using the Google Keyword Planner to Determine

Competitors

If you're in an ecommerce business you are going to have competitors that are trying to rank for keywords just like you are. It is likely that they developed their strategy using the Google Keywords Planner. Therefore, if you can use it to get some of the more popular search terms related to your particular niche, you'll be able to see what kind of competition is out there. All you have to do is type in something related to your keyword and then see what kind of keywords come up. You want to use the "Get Keyword Ideas" part of the planner and if you aren't familiar with how to use the tool, Google offers a comprehensive tutorial.

Checking Out the Competition

In either of these cases, you are going to end up with search results of companies that sell the same thing that you do. What you want to look for are actual ecommerce stores that sell products. If you come across a blog that happens to be talking about bandanas (or whatever your product is) and has Amazon affiliate items available in the sidebar, ignore it. You only want to evaluate ecommerce websites that are at least as serious as your web store.

Make a list of the competitors that pop up again and again when you try out various related keywords. Those companies – even if they don't sell the exact same thing you do – are going to be who you are competing against – at least for the most popular keywords. You might rank at the top of a search for a particular niche search (equine design bandanas anyone?) but that doesn't mean you are going to get traffic. You want to find out who is competing against you for keywords that will actually bring you traffic.

Evaluating That Competition

The last thing that you are going to do is decide how much of a threat this competition actually is to you. This is actually one of the easier things to do with the internet, because internet marketing is such a booming business that there are literally hundreds of thousands of marketing tools that will let you take a peek at what the other guys are doing.

© 2017 Raghu Ramasubbu

You might remember that a site's pagerank used to be a big deal. Now, it isn't necessarily an indicator of how strong a site is (although you can't discount it completely) and backlinks are the same way. You used to be able to tell exactly how you would be able to outrank a site by targeting the same keywords and getting more backlinks than they had.

Now, Google has changed their algorithm drastically. But you can still evaluate a company's strength by looking at some of the other factors that exist. For example: Google loves it when you have content on your website – and the more high quality content, the better. If you have a blog that published quality articles regularly, you'll be poised to be regarded as an expert in that particular field. The world of SEO and evaluating the strength of a website is an industry in itself, but if you learn what makes a website strong, you can make your site even stronger and rise above the competition.

MAKING YOURSELF UNIQUE AMONG YOUR COMPETITORS

So, you have learned how to identify your product, how to extrapolate a picture of your ideal customer archetypes and how to determine how strong the competition is in the particular niche you are trying to compete in. But how do you give yourself an advantage over all of those other people competing for the dollars being spent in your niche? That's actually not as complicated as you might think and it's not that difficult either. Plus, you'd be surprised how many ecommerce businesses out there actually fail to take this one important step.

Instead, these companies create "cookie cutter" or "clone" businesses that look like a pale imitation of whatever site they are trying to emulate. There's nothing wrong with trying to be successful like your favorite store, but there is something wrong with creating a website that looks almost exactly the same and sells the same products. You don't want to be a clone of a website that is selling; you want to be unique in the midst of these successful websites which will also make you successful. In other words, don't be a follower. Make your business into a trendsetting – a leader in the field and don't be afraid to take some chances. If you want to make your business stand out among the competition here are some ways to do exactly that.

Go Above & Beyond

If you want to make your company stand out among all of the others out there then you need to work harder than they are willing to work and that means giving more to your customers than other companies are willing to give. Whether that means manning your Twitter until the wee hours of the morning to do customer support, or paying for options that make the customer experience better, you'll find that companies that are willing to go the extra mile for their customers will end up with loyal buyers who will rarely go elsewhere, even if someone else has a better price. Whatever you do, don't be ordinary.

There are many 'average' companies out there that have nothing to make them stand out above the rest; be a mediocre company and you'll get mediocre sales.

Create a Winning Brand

If you want staying power in a competitive market, you need to make your brand stand out above all else. You want to make sure that you are the company that someone thinks about when they think about a product that you sell. Think about some of the most successful companies in the world for various products and services. Who do you think of when you think of fried chicken? Church's? KFC? What about when you think of tools and hardware? ACE is probably pretty high on your list. That's because these companies have created a winning brand. They have used advertising, marketing and plain old hard work to make themselves one of the top companies in the nation for that niche.

Make Your Marketing Memorable

You've heard of viral videos? Well, that's one of the most effective ways that people make their marketing memorable. Superbowl commercials are another way. The plan here is to create a marketing effort that is so successful at sticking in people's minds that they think of your brand later on, hopefully when they are in a position to buy a product or service that you offer. You don't necessarily have to create a viral video to make your marketing memorable (although if you can pull it off, that's an extremely effective method of getting your name out there) but you do need to make sure that every marketing effort you make is as memorable as you can design it.

Create a Compelling Blog

You've probably heard that a blog is one of the best ways to market your business. That is true for several reasons. First, the more content you have on your website, and particularly if you are publishing fresh content each week, the more authoritative your site becomes. Second, with each blog post that you create you target more keywords and if you can find a way to funnel the traffic that comes in via your blog posts over to your sales page, you will be turning those blog posts into cold, hard cash.

However, creating a blog isn't enough. You need to create a blog that people actually want to read. Publishing a boring blog post might get you some traffic to your blog with the keywords that you create, but it isn't going to make people stick around and read that blog post, nor is it going to make them want to head on over to your store and actually buy something. Also, a high bounce rate will make your credibility with Google and the other search engines go downhill.

Make Your Company an Expert in Your Field

If you want people to buy from your, make yourself an expert in the field you are in. For example, NAPA Auto Parts sells a lot of auto parts because people can go into any one of their parts stores and get expert advice on everything from which part they actually need to how to install it. If you are an expert in your niche, people will buy from you.

Develop a Unique Value Proposition

Having expertise in a field is important as is creating marketing that people will remember and a brand that they can put their trust in. But all of that is simply a precarious house of cards if you don't have anything of value to offer them. You want people to see the value in the products that you have, and that goes back to what we discussed in the first chapter – solving a problem for them.

Think of it this way: Imagine that you were sitting at your desk, with a ton of work to complete. Lunchtime rolled around and you were starving, but you didn't have time to go out and get something. Along comes a vendor selling a sandwich for $15. Sure, that's a pretty hefty price to pay for a sandwich, even a 12-inch sub sandwich, but you've got the money in your pocket and you're hungry, so you make the purchase. That's a unique value proposition. The vendor offered you something valuable that no one else was offering you.

Now imagine the same vendor coming along after you had ordered Chinese food delivery. You have already eaten and he comes along with his $15 sandwich. Not only do you not find value in his proposition, it is no longer unique, because another company has already met your need.

Cultivate Your "X-Factor"

Finally, you've heard of the "X-Factor." It is an indefinable quality that some companies have that makes people want to buy from them. There is no logic behind it like there are for more of the other items on this list. In fact, people often buy from an "X-Factor" company despite the lack of a good reason. Although cultivating that particular quality is difficult – because there are no instructions on how to do it, if you can pull it off you will be in a much more effective position to be successful at eCommerce.

PROMOTIONAL METHODS TO USE

Whether you are a startup or a seasoned eCommerce store, it's important to stay up to date with the most current marketing trends and techniques for your eCommerce business. In order to be successful in the digital commerce arena, it is crucial to invest in an effective website structure and marketing strategy.

If you're interested in finding out the best tried-and-true methods, as well as the newest techniques of marketing for an eCommerce business, pay attention to the 11 tips below.

Produce Original Content

Maintaining high quality web site content is critical to the success of digital commerce. It helps customers interact with you through the website whether it be communications, shopping or be part of a following as a loyal customer in the long run.

With the advent of Adobe Photoshop and numerous other photo editing tools, copying and re-engineering visual content has become possible in a matter of minutes. However, altered and duplicated material can be traced back to the original, which it creates an unimpressive image of the brand. It's better to spend the time and money to create or purchase original graphics, which will project your image in a positive light.

The same goes with textual content - Be creative. Be original.

Promoting original content is a great way to make a statement, strike a compelling idea, and make a mark on the user's mind. There is a fine line between content that engages users and content that deters them. Why not take an extra step, put in a little effort, and create something that will be genuinely compelling?

Give a Face to Your Business

Consumers have become the power player in the eCommerce industry, which means your business needs to stand out in a unique way. There is an abundance of companies that offer a large variety of products and services, giving customers the upper hand in making purchase decisions because they can play one company against another. People also have the ability to look up anything at any time with today's technology, which means you need to stay on top of trends, competitive pricing, and features in order to maintain a loyal customer base

Because of this, it's more important than ever to customize your user experience (UX) to cater to the needs of your audience. People don't want to shop or communicate with a faceless eCommerce website, lacking necessary components or a memorable tone. The key to an efficient UX design and implementation is user experience that would attract them back to the eCommerce site for repeat purchases. Capitalize on what makes your company, products, or services unique, and promote that inside a pretty package that is your eCommerce site.

Make your outreach efforts personal by taking the time to learn about your customers. People love it when they feel special, and if you make sure to add personal touches like addressing your prospects by name, sharing videos and pictures of your employees, and being transparent about your company processes and procedures, you will reap the benefits of a loyal customer base. All of this will add to the overall 'face of the business' and will hopefully make its way to the hearts of your customers.

Content Marketing

Content creation and marketing can attract new and repeat customers to your site. By creating and promoting original content, customers understand that you are an expert in that space and also keeping them abreast of the latest whether it be products, services or specials that are of interest to them.

There is an overload of content and information today. The effort that it takes to create original and quality content will eventually lead to customers being dazzled by your stories and perspectives.

Brainstorm with your team to create a list of the different types of content you wish to create, such as blog posts, videos, and newsletters. Also, make sure you are utilizing your marketing budget by consulting with experts, outsourcing work when necessary, and investing in high-quality software, subscriptions, employees, and training for your team. You will also find that if you work with the right people, many of the things you've paid for in the past can be done internally. Create diversity within your team and listen to everyone's ideas.

We also suggest that you create content based on Pareto's 80/20 rule, which means that your promotions should comprise of 80% informational content, and 20% promotional content. All of the content you publish should be relevant, interesting, and unique.

Sometimes it's okay to utilize content and materials that have worked in the past, but you must do so carefully. Make sure that it fits well, has not been overused, and presents value to the piece you are marketing. Also, edit reusable material when necessary so it adds as much value to your outreach as possible.

Social Media Marketing

Social media marketing is a very powerful tool that allows you to communicate with your industry, customers, and market in a personal way. You can utilize social media to generate engagement and interaction, boost traffic to your website, and develop a larger base of customers. Utilizing different social media platforms for different purposes also creates a rich presence for your company that diversifies your abilities, efforts, and will ultimately help you cater to your customers' needs in a way that grows your business over time.

Maintaining a solid tone and personality of your company through social media is very important because consistency is what will create trust within your audience. Ability to develop and maintain brand recognition and authority; there is a unified approach to quality and consistency of communication within your team. Building a brand requires effort and time and therefore it is critical that every employee works to maintain the brand strategy.

Make sure you are also using an analytics tool to measure how your social media efforts are impacting your bottom line. For this, give Mouseflow a try – their software tracks user activity on your website and provides you with visitor recordings, heatmaps, conversion funnels and form analytics. You can actually use this software to measure your social media results by finding users who visited your site from your Facebook or Twitter campaigns, filtering the funnel to see how visitors from different platforms are converting, and generating lists of users from social media for remarketing purposes. You can actually watch entire sessions and see everything your users are doing on your website!

Email Marketing

One of the most effective forms of reaching out to your customer base is through email marketing. Although you have to be very careful about the content within your emails and who is included in your outreach, the reason email marketing has been around for so long is because it works.

People have become habituated to junk email and often don't pay attention to emails that seem gimmicky or impersonal. They also are quick to mark emails as junk if the subject or content isn't closely related to their interests or if they feel they didn't "sign up" to be contacted via email.

In order to reach your audience most effectively, provide useful content within your emails. Make them as personal as you can, offer valuable promotions, and use it as an opportunity to socialize.

Open up about what your business is doing, any events you are attending, new features or products, and be transparent about your company. You want to relate to your customers on a level that gauges their interest and keeps them engaging with your emails.

Also, don't over-market by sending too many communications too often. People are busy enough as it is without having to go through countless emails from your company. Develop a consistent email marketing schedule that keeps your audience engaged, but not overwhelmed.

As always, make sure you are monitoring the analytics of your email marketing efforts. One great tool that can help you with this is the Google Analytics Dashboard, which is a free solution that gives you useful data about your email marketing efforts.

You can also track users who entered your website from your email campaigns with Mouseflow. All you have to do is set a custom URL that users "visit" when entering your site, and their entry page will contain that unique URL. A great way of doing this is to append UTM variables to your URL.

You can use Mouseflow filters or the search feature to find users whose sessions contained your custom URL. From here, you can save and export the list, perform analytics, and watch how they interacted on their site. You can also filter your heatmaps for this data to analyze how they engage with each page of your site, which elements they find most attractive, and more!

Lastly, make sure your emails have responsive layouts to accommodate every user and always send a test copy to yourself or trusted colleague that can point out last-minute errors.

Search Engine Optimization

One of the most important and manual methods of optimizing a successful eCommerce website is making sure it's optimized for search engines. With today's Search Engine Optimization (SEO) standards, it's now more important than ever to make sure your website is constantly updated with rich and relevant content, promotes a good user experience (UX), and is optimized to be as error-free as possible.

The content within your website should be rich, reliable, and provide information to the public that is useful and relevant to what they're looking for. For example, if you have an eCommerce store selling camping supplies, it's wise to provide detailed product information and possibly even host sections of your website that offer generous amounts of content that elaborates on the topics of camping, supplies, or related subjects. Using keywords within your content in a genuine way will also flag your website as a matching result in search engines when users are looking for something specific.

Good user experience (UX) optimization will also ensure a smooth flow throughout your website and will generate a positive quality rating within search engines. Make sure you are working with a good team

© *2017 Raghu Ramasubbu*

of developers to enhance your website as much as possible. The goal of UX design is to meet in the middle between business goals and customer needs. By doing this, you are making sure that they can easily find what they need from your website, and you are also providing a customer experience that can translate to purchase conversions.

Developers can also help you diagnose your website to find any problems or errors in the code. Tools like Mouseflow can flag areas of your website that are generating errors so that you can further analyze and fix them. If you are a Mouseflow client, try using the filters to search for click-error, which is automatically added to user sessions when a JavaScript error on your website is detected. When you generate a list of user sessions containing click-error, you can find patterns and share recordings, heatmaps, form or funnel analytics with your developers so that you can optimize your conversion rate and provide the best user experience possible.

Pay-Per-Click Marketing

There are three basic elements to any pay-per-click marketing campaign: the ad, the offer, and the landing page.

All three must be in good harmony and synchronization if you want to maintain the interest of the lead. The landing page must be a continuation of your ad, delivering what was promised as the reward of clicking on the ad, in order to take the visitor through your conversion funnel. It must also be customized for keywords to appear somewhere near the top of search engine results.

Keep the landing page free of distractions and unnecessary bells and whistles. Also, keep in mind that your landing page is the most appropriate place to boast your product benefits to the customer.

Optimize Your Marketing Efforts for Mobile

Devices

It is absolutely crucial to make sure your website is responsive to any user layout. Mobile users are starting to dominate the sea of internet use, and it's important to accommodate their needs to provide a good user experience (UX) for everyone.

People who visit your website do not want to be redirected to an app or web version of your website, they want the full-meal-deal. So, make sure you deliver what they are expecting and make the investment to enhance your website so that it's fully responsive.

You can also use mobile marketing techniques to target mobile users specifically. One of the most popular marketing trends is called geo-targeting, which advertises to mobile users based on their location. This technique enables you to reach out to customers who are within a specific distance of your business, and provide them with an incentive to stop by or make a purchase.

Target Wearable and VR Technology

Targeting wearable and Virtual Reality (VR) technology is a trending technique that grabs users in a new and exciting way. People are still getting used to this technology, and are not yet overwhelmed by or habituated to advertisements.

Your target audience for these mediums will be very refined, as these users are the part of the population that carries the latest technology at the palm of their hands at all times, keeps up to date with trends, and doesn't mind dropping some extra cash for items they desire. Although creating campaigns that are designed for these technologies can be expensive, the right approach can be worth the initial investment because a filtered audience is more likely to convert.

Make sure you are working with an experienced team who is up to date with the norms of this industry. By doing so, you can make sure your time and money is well-spent because you will ensure your campaigns are targeted and optimized for this technology. Keeping up with the latest trends and technology is extremely important in general, and even more so with this crowd of potential customers.

Launch Stores on Multiple Platforms

There are so many options available that allow you to integrate your business amongst a variety of platforms. Users are constantly engaging with social media, B2B networks, eCommerce sites, and other specialty areas of the internet. By hosting an eStore in their arena, you are making your business available to them and can nurture many different types of relationships, adding to your base of loyal customers.

Set up eStores on platforms like Facebook, Ebay, Amazon and Magento. There are many more out there, but the point is to make your company as available as possible to your target market. You can lead them from your eStore to your main website, if you so wish.

Retargeting

Retargeting is a technique that allows the eCommerce store to place ads on internet pages when a customer visits those sites. These are customers who have visited your website in the past, and the primary intent is to get them back to your stores by targeting these ads.

To effectively manage a retargeting campaign, make sure your ads are as specific as possible. Was the customer looking at a specific product? Make sure the ads displayed to them are ads of that specific product and link to the page of the product. Just like with Search Engine Optimization (SEO) and Pay Per Click (PPC) marketing, it's important to display the information the user is looking for the instant they click on your ad. If they click on an ad for hiking boots and are redirected to the home page of your camping website, they aren't going to be thrilled. But, if they are directed to the exact hiking boots they were considering, or even had added to their cart, before leaving your website, they will be much more likely to continue with a purchase.

In Conclusion

Staying current with the latest marketing trends and techniques is crucial for any successful eCommerce website. It's important to deliver relevant, interesting and valuable content and products that truly suite the needs of your target market. Reach out to your customers in a variety of ways and make sure you are working with a team of experts with varying skill sets. If you listen to everyone's ideas, you may find new ways of improving your current campaigns and outreach methods. The key to success is to track web analytics and ensuring optimum performance of the eCommerce web site pages.

With the right mix of marketing techniques, you can improve your conversion rate and create a sustainable business that will continue growing over time.

LAUNCHING YOUR ECOMMERCE STORE

For a one-person operation with limited inventory to sell, the ecommerce route doesn't have to be very complicated. If you plan to launch a business through which you hope to sell products via the Internet, you need a plan that covers every aspect from production to customer satisfaction. Leave out on step, and you may encounter difficulties in getting your business off the ground.

It is arguably a common misconception that setting up an online store is the ticket to quick money. While it's true that many businesses have achieved success in selling products via the Internet, a business is a business. When you are prepared with a financial plan, the means to produce and ship inventory, and quality customer service, you can watch profits rise. Ecommerce works similarly to the brick and mortar store - the only difference is that customers interact with you online.

ECOMMERCE PLATFORMS TO BUILD YOUR ONLINE STORE

Today, choosing the appropriate eCommerce platform for your business is much harder than ever before because of the increasing number of options you have. A good eCommerce platform will allow your company to make electronic exchanges on multiple devices, at anytime of the day with no hassle. Most websites are now accessible in a user-friendly format on all devices to guide the customer to checkout quickly. These newly upgraded eCommerce websites are the ones that are going to succeed because they were able to budget for a quality eCommerce platform & implementation that is the right fit for their unique business situation both now and in the future.

The eCommerce platform space has begun to mature and some of these platforms are now much more advanced than a decade old. How are you supposed to know which eCommerce platform is right for you? I think the first place to look is the trajectory and the data behind what businesses are currently using these eCommerce platforms. Are large companies using the platform? Are smaller companies using the platform successfully? Are the top websites using the platform? This data from Builtwith will help you decide whether the eCommerce platform is a good fit for your small, medium or enterprise size business.

WooCommerce

WooCommerce is a simple, easy to use, eCommerce platform for WordPress. WooCommerce is now responsible for 30% of all online stores, which is the largest market share out of any platform. WooCommerce is an extension to WordPress and is easy to install. It allows you to sell very quickly and easily with a WordPress website, as well as ship to wherever you'd like with free shipping or flat rate shipping.

WooCommerce is a great fit if you want to get a site up quickly, as well as utilize the incredible content management capabilities of WordPress such as native blogging capabilities and more. WooCommerce has a massive plethora of extensions to improve the software. It is an ideal fit for businesses just starting out in eCommerce or that have not yet hit the million plus online revenue threshold.

OpenCart

OpenCart is an easy to use lightweight eCommerce platform that is open source based on the PHP and MySQL technologies. It is more natively feature rich than WooCommerce but not nearly as impressive as the featured loaded Magento Community or Magento Enterprise platforms. It is a good fit for a new eCommerce business that wants to get up a site quickly at a low cost. It does not have as robust CMS capabilities as WordPress for non eCommerce content so it is a better fit if you have very little non eCommerce content.

Magento Community

Magento Community edition is the leading open source eCommerce platform among the top websites because it is built to provide online merchants with the most flexible cart system. Magento was developed in the year 2007 by the company Varien, and shortly released to the public just seven months later.

What makes Magento Community edition so impressive is that it comes with the features that most enterprise eCommerce platforms such as Demandware or Hybris would charge significant license fees for, at literally zero licensing cost. Features such as multi website, customizable order processing, complex catalog capabilities, and much more are native to Magento Community.

Magento Community edition is certainly the most powerful free open source eCommerce solution, especially with the newly enhanced 2.0 edition. However, with great power comes great responsibility. Magento Community is not to be taken

© *2017 Raghu Ramasubbu*

lightly and can become very expensive to maintain and customize just like any other enterprise & complex software.

Squarespace Commerce

Squarespace is a content management system which allows anyone to build and manage their brand online. They typically support both smaller companies and individuals such as local artists, as well as larger corporations looking to take their virtual businesses to the next level. Empowering individuals is something that Squarespace strongly believes in, by giving smaller brands the ability to stand out online with high quality customer support.

For non-coders, this web platform is highly recommended in order to get your website up and running because of its easy to use website builder tools. Squarespace is not open source, and is a hosted platform, therefore customization of the platform is limited. So if you are looking to make a more complex website with many features, you may want to look into other options. If you are an entrepreneur, local artist, or larger corporation with simpler website needs, Squarespace is for you.

Shopify

Shopify is a Canadian based eCommerce company developed in 2004, originally as an online store for snowboarding equipment. Simply enough, Shopify allows businesses to set up their online stores to sell their products to the public all with one monthly cost and infrastructure, opposed to the other open source platforms which require more work to setup. It is important to have multiple options and with this platform, there are more than a hundred different templates that Shopify offers when designing a website to make yours as personable and unique as possible.

There are plenty of templates that are modern and well designed free of charge. If you are a company that has a little bit of financial breathing room many high quality templates are $80-$180 that may pay off in the long run, seeing as it is just a single payment. Shopify is great for smaller retailers but is not necessarily a great fit for more complex eCommerce sites or B2B eCommerce needs. It does now offer a plus version for larger sites but doesn't seem to quite have the enterprise presence among larger sites that Magento, Demandware, Hybris, and other enterprise platforms have. Despite lack of enterprise market penetration, Shopify still shows healthy growth on all fronts.

Zen Cart

Out of all the platforms, Zen Cart was one of the first eCommerce web design platforms that offers free, user-friendly, open source shopping cart software. The online store management system was renovated in 2003 making a change by moving away from osCommerce and moving toward the newly coded template system which is largely CSS-based. The best thing about Zen Cart is you can download the system for free! They did this purposely because they wanted to stand out as a company that offers a technology that can be used by non-IT people. Zen Cart was once much more popular and has since lost market share to platforms like WooCommerce, Magento, Shopify and more. It has had a decreasing trajectory in usage for quite some time now.

OsCommerce

OsCommerce is an "Open Source" e-commerce solution that is available for free under the GNU General Public License. Having an open source model similar to Opencart, Magento, and Zencart allows users to access all the code and customize in order to change the aspects of the software to fit the needs of a business. OsCommerce was once very popular but has since lost marketshare to platforms that have become much modern in recent times such as Shopify and Magento. OsCommerce was started in 2000 as one of the first open source for eCommerce platforms.

BigCommerce

BigCommerce is an eCommerce software solution that helps businesses design their websites. They offer free premium templates depending on what you are trying to achieve. You don't need to have technical skills in order to build your website with BigCommerce which is helpful to many start-ups that are looking to dive into the eCommerce industry. There is a ton of flexibility when it comes to BigCommerce so whether you are selling 5 products or 5,000 products, you are still able to create the website that you desire, and because many start-ups begin at the lower end of the spectrum, this is a great ability to have.

Drupal Ubercart

The Drupal extension Ubercart gives your Drupal website the ability to sell online. Drupal, which is a leading open source content management system, allows users to access thousands of modules and themes in order to give as many personalized options as possible. As an open source eCommerce solution, Ubercart is a great platform to use if you are looking for great shopping cart functionality in tandem with the power of the Drupal CMS platform. An internal development team is able to alter the Ubercart features to accommodate many eCommerce needs because of Drupal's flexible open source architecture. Having flexibility is more important than most people realize when it comes to being successful with eCommerce.

When you are choosing which eCommerce platform you are most comfortable with, customer service, flexibility, and support are always improving at Ubercart. However, also keep in mind that the Ubercart platform marketshare seems to be shrinking despite the strong Drupal community.

Volusion

Volusion offers hundreds of free templates that are easy to implement to get your website up and running quickly. Volusion is a California based shopping cart solution, that integrates shopping cart software with product merchandising, site design, SEO, marketing and order processing. Also Volusion provides an affiliate marketing and rewards program called MyReward. This is a great feature for many small businesses because when customers are visiting and buying from your website, they can build loyalty points. These point eventually get transferred into a store credit, which is great for building long term relationships with consumers. Volusion was once a very popular platform but has since lost a lot of its momentum and market share to platforms like Shopify, BigCommerce, and Magento.

Big Cartel

This is a pretty basic online platform which is why this is one of the better platforms for companies selling a smaller range of products. Big Cartel has a range of options that are offered, one of them being free. The trick is with the free option you are only allow to showcase five of your products that you want to sell online. Now if you are a start up clothing company that has only five t-shirt designs so far, than Big Cartel could be exactly what you are looking for. Now if you are looking for a greater number than just five, you are more than welcome to choose from their budgeted options depending on the number of products you're looking to display.

nopCommerce

nopCommerce is a free, downloadable software. This very simple shopping cart solution could be great for new online businesses. You will notice that this platform allows your website to meet all of the search-engine standards such as search friendly URLs to well-structured content. It also has great themes for your products. nopCommerce is well known for its modular / layered structure which gives users the ability to create additional functionality and makes it as easy as possible to manage your websites. These layers are easily accessible and user friendly on a mobile device as well as on other alternative tablets.

Yahoo! Store

Yahoo! Stores is an eCommerce platform that allows you to choose from hundreds of free or paid templates for the development of an online site. It is known for being implemented for smaller companies because of its simplicity and low monthly cost similar to Shopify. The lowest rate can also be affordable by a almost any start-up as well. Yahoo! Stores plans are reflected by it's retailers expected monthly sales unlike say Shopify whose platform is based off the number of products being sold or the amount of storage a company needs for space to satisfy their website capabilities. Yahoo was once a very popular eCommerce platform but has since lost traction to companies like Shopify and BigCommerce.

Fotomoto

This Print-on-demand eCommerce system allows you to sell your artwork in multiple forms. Once you make an account and link it to wherever you had been selling them virtually in the past, it is very easy to get your site up and running without hassle. Behind the scenes of this platform are a handful of sales representatives, professional print labs, packaging and shipping services, and software specialist.

The great thing about Fotomoto is all the work the staff behind the curtains are doing on behalf of you and your business to make sure things run as smoothly as possible. One of those main selling points as a platform thats more directed at the website host (you) is the aftermath of the customers purchase. If you feel as though the easiest thing to do is too DIY, then by all means go ahead! But Fotomoto offers a printing network that prints, packages, and ships your order right to the customers for you! You don't have to lift a finger besides the one that you're using to complete the actual order. Fotomoto could be a great fit for smaller businesses looking to leverage a great print network like Fotomoto.

3D Cart

3D Cart is a software as a service eCommerce solution similar to Yahoo Stores, Bigcommerce, Shopify and more. This platform is great for any individuals that are looking to get their name and brand out into the virtual world of eCommerce. 3D Cart is known for its shopping cart solution which they claim powers over 17,000 stores, although that data is not backed up by Builtwith. You are able to choose from hundreds of themes and templates that 3D Cart has to offer.

Selling products on Facebook, as well as promoting your products videos on Youtube is easier than ever with 3D Cart. With the Facebook app as well as having a sleek Omnichannel platform, your entire website should look the same across all devices and channels. When your website is complete, you are going to want to start promoting it! You are able to promote your store by email marketing, as well as mobile commerce tools, and social media integration with 24/7 hour assistance from the 3D Carts customer service line.

Miva Merchant

Miva is a long standing eCommerce platform for small and medium size businesses. It is great for up and coming businesses because it is a versatile and stable platform that is able to be customized for whatever kind of look your company is going for. They have a less expensive small business version starting at less than $100 a month and a more expensive enterprise edition that goes for approximately $1500 a month. Miva provides a full range of in house services to help businesses implement their solution rather than going through a third party.

X-Cart

X-cart is an eCommerce shopping cart site that allows you to choose from either a cloud-based cart or a self-hosted licensed software option. Within these two options your company is able to pick from a handful of attributes such as web design, migration, installation, hosting, online monitoring, and fraud services. It has a much smaller eCommerce community than many of the other small business platforms but still has thousands of sites using the platform.

E-Junkie

E-Junkie is a shopping cart service that is set up for business owners and operators who are looking to enter into the Commerce world. This software prides its self on the security of their transactions. All transactions through e-Junkie are done within their system which can be embedded into your website. Customers who purchase virtual goods from a client's E-Junkie store will then receive a secure downloadable link that expires after a certain number of downloads or a certain time.

E-Junkie is an interesting solution because it essentially allows you to add their shopping cart into your website via code snippets. They support many payment gateways like Paypal as well as have integrations with platforms like Google Analytics.

Drupal Commerce

Drupal is used by larger companies and organizations. This platform is increasing in usage but at a much slower rate relative to WordPress & WooCommerce because it is significantly more expensive to implement and maintain. If you have very complex content related website needs but also need eCommerce, Drupal Commerce could be a good solution for your website.

Magento Enterprise

Magento Enterprise edition comes straight from the Magento Community edition and has the same base core files as Magento Community. Magento Enterprise has many features such as rewards points, customer segmentation and more that Magento Community does not. Magento Enteprise is a very successful platform because it is less expensive than some of the major enterprise platforms like Hybris and Oracle Commerce but has the capabilities to compete with such platforms. The other advantage is that there is a large pool of developers and agencies that support it because of its massive community edition usage.

Demandware

Demandware is an enterprise cloud-based eCommerce platform technology for retailers. This software allows them to make and manage a custom online website as well as give them full access to the mobility feature. Demandware is a public company that has become very successful by doing a revenue share model with customers. It is in the enterprise class tier as one of the more expensive eCommerce solutions on the market.

Hybris

Hybris is an omni-channel eCommerce platform that integrates all digital and physical customer touch points into a single platform. It is now owned by SAP, a global leader in information technology solutions. This worldwide managed company is a leader in both B2B and B2C eCommerce industries by keeping up with the everyday changes in the Internet world. It is a best in class eCommerce solution that is on the more expensive enterprise side to implement for larger companies.

Oracle Commerce

Oracle Commerce was an add on to the companies successful CX portfolio. Oracle Commerce was originally ATG Commerce which was acquired by Oracle a few years ago. Now, Oracle Commerce continues to power some of the largest sites in the world. Similar to IBM, Demandware, and Hybris, it is on the more expensive side of eCommerce platforms.

IBM WebSphere Commerce

This single, unified software platform framework is built for enterprise eCommerce websites. IBM WebSphere Commerce provides an omni-channel shopping experience that helps engage your customers with experiences through great content, marketing, and promotions. IBM Websphere powers some of the largest eCommerce sites in the world and is typically a fit for larger complex sites that require extensive customization. If you do not have a large implementation budget, IBM Websphere is probably not for you.

NetSuite eCommerce

SuiteCommerce enables businesses to seamlessly connect every step of a multi-channel, multi-location business — from ecommerce, POS and order management to merchandising, marketing, inventory, financials and customer service. This platform allows you to create unique, personalized and compelling mobile, web and in-store experiences that differentiate your brand and exceed customer expectations. One of the biggest advantages of Netsuite is the ability to have an all in one backend ERP, CRM, seamlessly connected with your eCommerce platform all together.

Digital River

Digital River offers eCommerce, payments and top online marketing services to global companies of all sizes. Known as an Commerce-as-a-Service solution, being able to support the shopper experience at its best is something that Digital River prides its self on. Local shopping experiences in global markets and more payment options than any other company makes Digital River a leading global provider. What differentiates DR is their full solution: reseller business model; robust, flexible cloud-based SaaS platform; and comprehensive business operation support which manages, supports, and powers users sites. They typically provide eCommerce services for larger websites not small businesses.

GSI Commerce (eBay Enterprise)

Formally known as GSI Commerce, eBay Enterprises provides a globally well developed eCommerce solution and service that allows you to be ultra connected to your consumers at all times. This company specializes in running online shopping sites for larger brick and mortar brands and retailers. There are not many GSI Commerce sites in existence today as the platform is not as popular as it once was.

STEPS TO DO AFTER CHOOSING YOUR DESIRED PLATFORM

Get a Domain

You will want to choose a domain name which rhymes with your store name to make your business unique and it wouldn't cost you more than $13 per year. You will need to set this up once you decide if you want to invest further money into your business. It is important to note, however, that a custom internet address provides social accountability when you start advertising your site, which can increase your sales significantly. To buy a domain, go to goDaddy, Namecheap and follow the instructions shown.

Choosing your Hosting Platform

You will be needing a host server should it be you aren't using platforms like Shopify or Bigcommerce. This means you will be the one hosting your website;

you can as well get a website developer to assist you with the task.

Choose Your Store Theme

Go to the Theme Store for whichever platform you have chosen and choose a theme. There are numerous free themes if your budget is tight. Try choosing the one that requires the least changes to make it look like you want. Editing your theme is a time consuming task and often ends in a website with lots of mistakes. A few popular selections are New Standard, Supply, Simple. Once you have found your preferred store look, click the Preview button In Your Store, and install it to your store

How to Tweak Your Theme: Wordpress, bigcommerce, and Shopify are non-programmer friendly. To edit your store look, just go to Online Store, Themes, Customize Theme. On the right-hand sidebar you'll see each section of your theme: Header, Body, Footer, etc. Open each section and play around to get the feeling of what can be done with the theme.

© *2017 Raghu Ramasubbu*

There's nothing specific you need to change, but it's good know what you can do if you ever want any customization.

Add Your Logo

Your store logo is likely to be the first element seen by your store visitors, but a logo made by a professional graphic designer can cost you a lot of time and money. That's why Shopify has created a easy to use and absolutely free Logo Maker. Just go to Shopify Logo Maker, enter your brand name and test out some variations until you get a decent looking logo.

Have Your Standard Pages Ready

Content is extremely important. This is an area that you should focus on and spend more time on in the future.

—However, the following sections should be enough to start with: About Us, Terms &

Conditions, Privacy & Returns Policy, Shipping & Delivery Information, and Contact Us. To create a page, go to Store dashboard, search for the Page section, and click Add Page.

—About Us Page: This page eventually needs to be unique, but this will take quite a bit of time. In the meantime, copy and paste one of the pre-generated 'About Us' pages from the list below and edit it to suit your store later.

—Shipping & Delivery Information: Most of the sellers on Oberlo have very similar delivery prices and timeframes, so it is best to copy and paste this standardized shipping & delivery page.

—Contact Us: Keeping in close contact with your customers is very important. Make sure you place a clearly visible 'Contact Us' link on your store. To create a contact page, click the Add

New Page button and change the page template to contact

—Required Policies: If you are using Shopify, it offers a handy tool for generating terms and conditions, standard privacy, and return policies. Just go to Shopify Settings, Checkout, and scroll down to the Refund, Privacy, and TOS statements section to generate each policy sample.

Add a Payment Gateway

Add your PayPal email address under the Shopify Settings, Payments Section. Later, you can change, remove, or add additional payment options. If you don't have a PayPal account, registration at PayPal.com will take about 5 minutes.

Adjust Shipping Settings

The sourcing tool we will recommend to you will offer most of the products with a free delivery option.

So I suggest adding a free shipping rate for all of your orders, as well. For example, go to Shopify Settings, Shipping, and delete all shipping zones that are noninternational, and edit the international zone rate to Free. You can later adjust your shipping rates to include more delivery options. But Free Shipping is enough for now.

Set Up Your Billing Information

Before launching your store you should enter your billing information. You won't be charged until your Trial Ends (14 days). For example, just go to your Shopify Settings, Account and enter your Billing information

POINTS TO CONSIDER TO LAUNCH YOUR FIRST ECOMMERCE WEBSITE

A number of studies have shown that a large percentage of modern users prefer mobile commerce apps to ecommerce websites. Hence, your ecommerce website must deliver optimal user experience to beat competition and mobile commerce. You have to consider several factors to make the web store keep visitors engaged and seduce them to buy the products/services. In addition focusing the look, feel, features, and functionality of the website, you also need to explore ways to optimize its user experience. To optimize the user experience delivered by the website, you need to enhance its accessibility, usability, security, credibility and search engine visibility.

© 2017 Raghu Ramasubbu

10 Points to Consider while Launching Your First Ecommerce Website

1. User

While planning and developing your first ecommerce website, you must focus extensively on the users and their choices. You must remember that a web store does not allow customers to touch, feel or smell the products physically. Hence, you must keep the users engaged by making their shopping experience fast and hassle-free. You can always keep the visitors engaged by offering products at discounted prices, providing free shipping, and keeping the shopping and checkout process simple.

2. Design

You also need to focus on the design and user interface of the ecommerce website to impress and engage visitors effectively. Unlike established brands, you need to explore ways to gain the trust and confidence of visitors. Hence, you have to include a number of elements in the website design - a recognizable logo, shopping deals, product options, product review and testimonials, and call to action. At the same time, you need to ensure that the look and feel of the ecommerce website is both intuitive enough to keep the purchase process simple and straightforward.

3. Mobile Optimization

As mentioned earlier, a large percentage of modern users prefer mcommerce (mobile commerce) apps to ecommerce websites. Likewise, most people nowadays access eCommerce websites on their smartphones, tablets or phablets. Hence, you need to ensure that the ecommerce website delivers optimal user experience on both computers and mobile devices. You can always opt for responsive web design to make the web store look good on each device with a single code base. The mobile optimization will further enhance the website's visibility on major search engine results pages (SERPs).

4. Social Elements

You need to include many social elements in the eCommerce website to impress the users. The users must have option to share the products purchased from your web store with their friends through popular social networks. Also, the social elements will help users to promote your new ecommerce website and enhance its popularity. You can even use the social elements as an efficient tool to gather information about customers and track their behaviour.

5. Search Box

No ecommerce site can display all its products on a single page. But you can always impress visitors by displaying branded goods to the visitors initially. Also, you must allow customers to check your products based on specific criterions or categories.

The website must allow visitors to search and find the relevant products without any delay or hassle. Hence, you need to ensure that your ecommerce site includes a robust search box. The search box will enable users to find a specific product and buy it directly, without browsing through an array of products.

6. Shopping Cart

Your choice of shopping cart will have a direct impact on the user experience delivered by the ecommerce portal. You have option to choose from an array of open source and commercial shopping carts written in different programming languages. But you must opt for a shopping cart software that enables users to check their previous and current purchases quickly and conveniently. Also, the shopping cart must allow users to add or remove items without any hassle. At the same time, you also need to enhance the accessibility and visibility of the shopping cart by using the commonly used simple basket icon.

7. Payment Options

The choice of online payment option varies from one customer to another. Some customers prefer making payment through their debit/credit cards or internet banking facility, while others opt for popular online payment options like PayPal and digital wallets. Hence, you need to ensure that each customer can make payment for the products purchased by him/her with any payment option. At the same time, you also need to keep the online payment and financial transactions of customers secure by using a reliable payment gateway and the latest encryption techniques.

8. Trust Marks

You must remember that a large percentage of people are sceptical about new eCommerce websites. Hence, you must explore ways to enhance the eCommerce website's credibility and win the trust of customers. In addition to including robust security features in the web store, you also need to display the accreditation

© 2017 Raghu Ramasubbu

certificates and trust marks of reputed brands. The trust marks and accreditation certificates will enhance the credibility of your newly launched web store. The trust marks will further assure customers that their personal data will remain private and online transactions will remain 100% secure.

9. Option to Answer Pre-Sale and Post-Sale Questions

While buying products from a new ecommerce website, users often ask a variety of question before and after the purchase. Hence, you must answer the pre-sale and post-sale questions of customers immediately increase your sales and revenue. Like other websites, you can answer the pre-sale and post-sale questions of customers through either online chat or phone call. But the customer must be able to see the options available to answer questions. You need to ensure that the phone number or online chat option is clearly visible to each customer. Also, you must deploy skilled customer care executives to answer the pre-sale questions of website visitors appropriately and convert them into customers.

10. Search Engine Visibility

You can easily divert regular search engine traffic to the eCommerce website by complying with the guidelines recommended by popular search engines like Google and Bing. For instance, Google ranks websites based on metrics like mobile friendliness and load time. Also, it recommends entrepreneurs to build web stores with responsive web design. While planning the ecommerce website, you must keep in mind the guidelines and recommendations of major online search engines. The search engine optimized design will help you to get regular website visitors without launching expensive digital marketing campaigns in the future.

SCALING AND OPTIMIZE YOUR ECOMMERCE BUSINESS

Ecommerce success can be accurately measured using seven metrics: Conversion Rate, Shopping Cart Abandonment Rate, Cost of Acquiring Customer, Repeat Customer Rate, Average Order Value, Customer Lifetime Value, and Payment Approval Rate. Learn what these metrics measure and simple strategies on how to improve them.

Conversion Rate (CR)

A high conversion rate should be a major focus for any ecommerce business, because a high conversion rate means that a large portion of people visiting your site are finalizing a purchase. Many factors can lower your conversion rate, but arguably the most frustrating factor of a low CR is Shopping Cart Abandonment.

Shopping Cart Abandonment Rate (SCAR)

Shopping cart abandonment is when a customer adds items from your ecommerce site to their online shopping cart but never finalizes the purchase. Conversion rates lowered by shopping cart abandonment are likely to be caused by a poor checkout experience or an inability to process the customer's payment method.

Cost of Acquiring Customer (CAC)

Cost of acquiring customer measures the total cost of driving a customer to convert throughout the acquisition funnel, anything from promoting clicks or impressions on Facebook to purchasing ad space on Google. If this measurement is anywhere close to your CLTV, you should rethink your marketing strategy to lower costs and increase effectivity by targeting the right audience.

Repeat Customer Rate (RCR)

Repeat customer rate is the percentage of customers that return to your site to make another purchase. A higher RCR means you have more loyal customers that will help promote your good or service and ultimately bring in more consistent revenue. If the RCR is too low, this could be a sign that people are dissatisfied with the final product and are unwilling to return.

Average Order Value (AOV)

Average order value is the average price of an order on your website per customer. This metric helps you keep track of incoming revenue from current traffic and conversion rates. You can raise the AOV by increasing the average ticket price of your product; however, you should consider how much customers are willing to pay for your product.

Customer Lifetime Value (CLTV)

Customer lifetime value measures the value of an average customer throughout their entire relationship with your company. Conceptually, CLTV incorporates the metrics of Average Order Value, Cost of Acquiring Customer, and Repeat Customer Rate. The AOV directly affects the purchase value of the customer, the CAC affects the total revenue you attain from the customer, and the RCR affects the timespan that the customer remains loyal to your business. When calculating CLTV you must consider your AOV, CAC, and RCR performance.

Payment Approval Rate (PAR)

Payment approval rate is important because it measures the health of the business payment engine. Generally approval rate is low (about 10-30%) for cross-border ecommerce merchants that sell to Latin America because they are unable to process local card payments. With local payment methods and local/multiple acquiring, the approval rate trends to increase by up to 80-90%.

How to Improve Your eCommerce Performance

1. Improve CLTV & RCR: Focus on Retaining Customers

According to the White House Office of Consumer Affairs, it costs 6-7 times more to attract a new customer than to keep an existing customer that has already purchased from you before. Placing more focus on delighting returning customers can help your business retain a steady revenue without having to spend extra money on acquisition strategies.

2. Lower CAC: Target Potential Customers Accurately

Acquisition of a customer can be costly, especially when considering the many strategies used across social media and search engine platforms such as Facebook and Google. Lower these costs by targeting your audience accurately. Know what platforms your potential customers use more often, what topics they search for on the internet, and how to commucate to them best.

3. Lower SCAR & Increase PAR: Optimize Payment Methods and Checkout Experience

Shopping cart abandonment usually occurs because the potential customer is dissatisfied with their experience toward the bottom of the funnel. Make sure your checkout process is smooth, easy, and secure. A great example is the one-click checkout feature offered by Amazon. Other major cause of a high cart abandonment rate is a lack of payment options; consider offering local payment methods to accept more payment types and increase conversion rates.

4. Increase CR & CLTV: Improve User Experience

Work on continuously improving your user experience, by doing so potential customers will be attracted to your website, stay on your webpage longer, and will be more likely to convert. A positive user experience coupled with a positive product experience, will achieve higher CR & CLTV values.

MAKING YOURSELF A NICHE EXPERT

One of the things that you are going to have to do to make yourself successful in your eCommerce efforts is to choose a niche and make yourself an authority for that niche. We'll explore what becoming an authority on a particular niche actually means and why it is so important to selling products, as well as some of the ways that you can do it. But first, let's define what a niche expert is.

What are Niche Experts?

When it comes to retail, niche experts are those websites where people go to buy products in that niche because they trust the niche expert. A niche expert is a website that ranks high in Google for particular niche keywords and who can be found being recommended on social media and word-of-mouth and who other websites link to when someone asked who they should ask a question about that niche. Niche experts are websites that have a reputation for knowing the niche that they are in and being able to provide not only great products in that niche, but also support for the products, recommendations and a high degree of trust.

Why Should You Make Yourself a Niche Expert?

Obviously, there are a number of advantages to become a niche expert but the most important one is that you will make more money. People want to buy from someone who is an expert in a particular niche. Many people would rather buy from a name that they know and trust rather than a site that sells just about everything. That's why there are people who still shop at Best Buy and other electronic stores online or buy their computer parts from Newegg rather than Amazon. They know that the retailer is an expert in the products that they are buying and can trust their recommendations, or the products they have listed.

There are other reasons that you should make yourself an expert in your niche as well. For one thing, you'll rank higher as a result of the links that you get and the reputation you achieve as an authority site. Google will recognize this from various telltale signs, and will give you more ranking juice. Also, people will want to link to you, so you'll get traffic from those sources directly as well. Also, when you have an authority site, it is very easy to expand into other related areas. For example: if a website is considered an authority on shoes, they will rank higher and easier if they expanded into clothing than a new website that was devoted just to clothing would.

How to Make Your eCommerce Site into a Niche

Expert Site

So, how do you create an authority site within your niche that will give you all of the benefits mentioned in the last paragraph – being able to rank higher in Google, getting more links to your site and more sales because people consider you an authority? It isn't all that difficult but it does take some time and a great deal of hard work. There are two types of authority, page authority and domain authority, but for the purposes of ecommerce site you should be concentrating on domain authority.

Linking Strategies to Build Authority

The first thing you need to do if you want Google to consider you an authority site is to tell them what is it you do; they aren't going to ask so when the spiders come crawling you want to have your website's internal linking strategy in place where you can show Google what sort of topics you are an authority in.

You do this by creating strong bonds between the pages of your site. Each page should be optimized for a specific keyword or group or keywords and then linked to from deep links within your site. That means linking topics of the same type to each other. For example, if you have 10 products that are tools or hardware, on each page for those ten, you want to put something like a "related products" widget beneath it.

That's the great thing about Shopify: it makes tasks like this very easy to do. You should also create a page that lists all of the products within that particular topic and then make sure that Google knows this is your "Daddy" page for the child products that it lists by making sure that you link to that page 3-4 times more than you link to a specific product page.

These "Daddy" pages are going to become the authority figures of your site, with Google understanding that whatever topic these pages are about, that topic is something that your site might be an authority on. So, suppose your site was about hardware and you had a page for hammers and another for saws. You would be ranked more highly for hammers and saws than any other tool that comes up, even if you sell that particular tool. Also, make sure that you are linking to these "Daddy" pages from your 'About' page, contact page, footer or other areas in your site than just your product pages.

The next part of building your authority is getting links from outside sites – not owned or frequented by you – with the link containing keywords that are related to your site topic somehow. Now, you're going to get some of these naturally, especially if people think you know what you're talking about and can be trusted to recommend a product or service in that niche. But to begin with, you might have to send some of those links your way on your own. The way that you do that is by writing or publishing related content on other sites, or simply finding a site that is willing to link to you. Note that an inbound link doesn't mean much to Google if it doesn't come from a site that is related to your topic in some way, or is from a massive authority website.

Creating Video Content

Creating video content is another great way to get your name out there as well as get some traffic to your store. If you can make an expert video showing that you know what you're talking about, and it gets views on YouTube or another video-sharing site, you'll get traffic coming to your store, as long as you provide a link for them to navigate there. If you feel comfortable creating video content, this is a great way to go.

Google's Own Recommendations on Building an

Authority Page

Google has actually recommended that you ask yourself these questions when trying to create an authority site. If the answer is NO to any of these questions, you probably need to fix it.

1. Is your content original, not like anything else on the web and definitely not plagiarized?
2. Is your advice practical? Are you advising people looking for a mortgage to get a "Construction for Dummies" book and build it themselves to save money?
3. Did you correct all of the misspellings, grammatical errors and typos?
4. Is the information that you're providing valuable? Providing obvious information will not make you an authority site.
5. Is the article cluttered?
6. Would you bookmark your page?

IMPROVING YOUR ECOMMERCE STORE

The Technical Stuff

1. Url Structure

Static, descriptive URLs are key to a good ecommerce website. You want URLs that a person can look at and understand what the page is about, and that gives the search engines an idea as to what your page is about as well.

Your URLs should be descriptive, concise, and unique. A good URL structure for an ecommerce site will generally look like this:

Domain.com/category-name/sub-category/product-name

If you have optimized category and product names, and you're auto-generating your URLs, you'll have well optimized URLs by default.

2. Auto-Generated Urls After Page Edits

Some content management systems (CMS) get a little sloppy with URLs when it comes to page edits. Some automatically auto-generate URLs if a product name changes, and other will append -1, -2, etc. to URLs after making changes to the content of the page. If your CMS is doing this, you're going to start generating a bunch of URLs for the same page, the very definition of duplicate content. Talk to your website development team ASAP to get an override in place so that changes to your products do NOT generate new URLs.

3. Sort Order Parameters & Pagination

If you've got a great ecommerce website with lots of products and a focus on user experience, you will have a few different ways to filter and display your products. Often, all those great sort and filter options end up in your URLs…

https://www.domain.com/category/l/price:100-200?dir=asc&limit=24&order=name
http://www.domain.com/category.html?dir=asc&limit=24&order=production_time

And if you're Amazon, sometimes that filtered data URL looks like this:

http://www.amazon.com/s/ref=sr_nr_p_n_feature_browseb_0?fst=as%3Aoff&rh=n%3A7141_23011%2Cn%3A10445813011%2Cn%3A7147440011%2Cn%3A1040660%2Cn%3A1045024%2Cn%3A2346727011%2Cp_89%3AO%27Neill%2Cp_n_feature_browsebin%3A11006713011&bbn=10445813011&ie=UTF8&qid=1462220_86&rnid=11006712011

The best way to handle these is with canonicalization. Adding a canonical tag to your pages can help the search engines identify which page is the "main" one, and which bloated URLs should be ignored. Google has more info on how to best add canonical tags here.

4. Redirecting Old Urls

After you remove old products/categories from the site and clean up those auto-generated URLs you'll need to redirect the old URLs to the new ones. Any URLs that you do not plan on using again should be 301 redirected to the most relevant URL. For ecommerce websites the easiest way to do this is to redirect products to their parent category.

Domain.com/category-1/product-name.html

Would redirect to:

Domain.com/category-1/

Then, if someone follows an old link to the site they end up on a page that is still relevant to what they were looking for instead of getting a 404 page.

Speaking of 404 error pages….

5. 404 Error Page

If someone follows a link to a page that no longer exists, has a link with a typo, or otherwise tries to access a URL that doesn't resolve they will get a 404 error page. If this is a generic "page not found" error your user will click "Back" and leave your site. However, if you deliver them to a page that is functional and engaging, you can use this opportunity to keep them on your site.

Your error page should have:
—Main Navigation
—Search Bar
—Contact Line
—Social Media Links

You can also have a lot of fun with your error page and make it really unique to your brand. A good example of this is Lego, who have made their error page fun, though not fully optimized for ecommerce.

6. Robots.Txt

You want the crawlers to come and eat up every single page on your site, right?

Nope! Leverage your Robots.txt file to block crawlers from accessing checkout pages, account info pages, and other restricted pages. Do let them crawl your images (yay image search!) and definitely let them crawl your product warranty pages and shipping info pages because people like to search for those things, too.

7. Page Load Time

Have you checked your page load time lately? More than just your home page? What about your mobile site?

Use a tool like Pingdom or Google PageSpeed Insights to make sure that your pages are still super speedy. Better yet, use Google's Search Console to double check which pages Google is reporting as being slow. Page speed is not only important for user experience (UX) but it's also a Google ranking factor so make sure your website is lickety split.

7. XML Sitemap

Check if your CMS can generate an XML sitemap for you. If it can, save that that as sitemap.xml (located at www.domain.com/sitemap.xml) and then submit it to Google via Google Search Console.

If it can't, there are several free XML sitemap generators out there that can help do the job.

9. Schema.Org Markup

Schema markup lets you clearly identify all the key points of your website to the search engines. Product names, sizes, prices, reviews, etc. can all be clearly pointed out to Google when the bots come to crawl

© *2017 Raghu Ramasubbu*

your site. Google then uses this data in their search results, often resulting in enhanced listings.

On-Site & Content Issues

10. Content Length & Quality

A common issue with ecommerce sites is not having enough content on the home page and on category pages. Your product descriptions are extremely important but so are your category pages, as these are the pages that will rank for shorter tail keywords. If you don't have a content area on your category pages, add one!

11. Navigation Structure

If you have a large database of products, it is absolutely essential that you have a slick navigation structure. People need to know where they are at all times so they can continue to navigate the site. Otherwise, they'll either revert back to the home page or just leave the site entirely.

Let's check out Amazon, who clearly has the navigation issue down. On a site with billions of products across multiple categories, they've broken down their navigation to smaller pieces to make it relevant to the category you are viewing, while still allowing you to access the rest of the site.

12. Internal Site Search

Even if your navigation is super amazing, people will skip all those clicks and dive right into the site search. These visitors know exactly what they are looking for and don't want to mess around. You need to give them what they want right away so that they can complete their transaction.

All too often site search is not given proper attention and you miss out on sales because visitors literally cannot find what they are looking for. Checking your website analytics for internal site queries (more: info on how to set up Site Search tracking in analytics) can help to identify site search shortcomings. If your

© *2017 Raghu Ramasubbu*

internal site search functionality isn't up to par, or if you have a large database of products, you might want to consider investing in a tool like Nextopia that provides auto-complete, let's you filter product results, and more, to help you better merchandize your search results.

13. Heading Tags

Typically, your heading tags should the the product name on product pages and category name on category pages.

Heading 1 <h1> is the MOST important content of the page. It's the page title, what the page is all about. For products, it's the name of the product:

Heading 2 <h2> are your sub-headings. Heading 3 <h3> are your sub-sub-headings.

Technically you can drill down deeper to sub-headings but really, if you're going that deep do

© *2017 Raghu Ramasubbu*

they really count as important headings on this page anymore?

14. Keyword Use

SEO 101: Use the keywords you want to rank for and that are 100% relevant to your business.

15. Content Links

Your products are probably all a little bit related, right? If you have one product that goes great with another, let your visitors know! Link to the cookies page on your milk page. Link to your sunscreen category in your beach chair product description. Internal links are a great way to up-sell while building some good internal links with descriptive anchor text.

16. Page Title Tags & Meta Description Tags

These are important because they show up in the search results. They're a first point of contact with your potential visitor so you want to make them great.

17. Images & Alt Text

Who loves image search? You do!

Lots of people search Google Images for items that they want to buy. Maybe it's an item that they can't remember the name of but would recognize to see. Or maybe it's an item that there is lots of variation for and they want to find the right image before clicking back and forth into different websites. Like finding the right pair of custom fairy wings or throwback basketball shoes.

Make sure you optimize all of your images; both image name and image alt tag to start ranking in that sweet image search traffic.

18. Mobile Site

Ensuring that your website experience, checkout process, and forms are all mobile optimized will help get those sales. If someone is having a hard time making a purchase on their device they might wait until later… or more than likely they'll move on to another site or just forget about that purchase entirely.

Run your URL through Google's Mobile-Friendly Test to make sure it's being reported as "Mobile Friendly":

https://www.google.com/webmasters/tools/mobile-friendly/

Also make sure you are checking analytics for insight on the actual use of your mobile website.

19. Blog

"Blog posting is a waste of time. I'm not generating sales from blog posts." – Website owners who miss the point.

Writing blogs about celebrity engagements likely won't give you a direct boost in engagement rings. But what it will do is bring in more search traffic for a wider variety of keywords and will help to build brand awareness, search traffic, links to the site - all of which will lead to building website authority. Then, when that searcher IS ready to buy an engagement ring (or drop some really serious hints about which one they want on Pinterest) your brand is already a familiar one and your engagement ring posts and photos will be the ones aggressively shared until a decision is made.

Off-Site Optimization

20. Shopping Data Feeds

Are you sharing your data feeds on shopping networks? No? You're missing out.

Generating a shopping feed is (usually) fairly easy and can bring you some serious wins with increasing your audience reach. As a cost-per-click program it's also one of the more affordable marketing platforms as visitors are quite qualified before they click through to you.

"Google Shopping is the top performer, highest traffic and conversion rate shopping site for merchants online – consistently generating more clicks and sales for retailers." – Search Engine Watch

21. Social Media

Social media can lead to sales. Make sure you're take advantage of upcoming holidays, what's trending, hash-tagging your brand, and getting involved in the conversation. Including your audience in on games, contests, and insider offers can help to increase brand loyalty as well.

Pop Quiz: Which social platform tends to drive the largest average order? Answer: YouTube!

Video production costs have dropped dramatically and it's easy to create cheap, quick videos on your phone. The important thing is to remember your audience: use the platform that best speaks to your audience and what they need to facilitate the sale.

SOME THINGS TO AVOID

There are some specific niches that should be approached with great caution. We recommend you to think twice if you want to try them.

Items that are usually carefully checked before the purchase include sophisticated electronics, footwear, exquisite clothing, etc. When we buy such products in regular brick-and-mortar shops, we try them out first and make sure they suit us by all parameters. If you include such offers in your store, be ready to deal with lots of product refunds and returns – most likely, your customers will experience some difficulties with ordering the right modification from the first time.

Items that can get damaged during transportation. Fragile products made of glass, porcelain, etc., as well as food, are not particularly suitable for being loaded in and out multiple times. Since the delivery can take a good deal of time, the overall condition of such items by the moment when the package is received can be quite disappointing for the customer and, therefore, quite harmful for your store reputation.

Items that can possibly experience some legal issues while being taken by a postal service and transferred through customs. Knives, fishing and hunting guns,

© *2017 Raghu Ramasubbu*

bows and arrows, etc. can be classified as questionable goods by a postal service and customs; therefore it is vital to check their requirements beforehand to be absolutely sure you will not experience any troubles before shipment. Please note that these requirements vary in different countries, so take some time to learn more about these issues in your target region.

Large and heavy items. Huge packages may cause some undesirable shipping issues. At the very least, the cost of such a delivery will be frustratingly high, and your customers will see no point in ordering such an item instead of buying it in a regular store.

This is the exact way we select niches for our clients who want to start their own drop shipping stores. Every webstore is created based on the results of such an in-depth analysis, and we do our best to make our customers satisfied with the financial outcome.

www.ingramcontent.com/pod-product-compliance
Lightning Source LLC
Chambersburg PA
CBHW051309220526
45468CB00004B/1266